D1218238

SHAPING THE FUTURE

Community-Based Residential Services and Facilities for Mentally Retarded People

Edited by

Philip Roos, Ph.D.
Executive Director

Brian M. McCann, Ph.D.
Director, Research and Demonstration Institute

and

Max R. Addison, M.S.
Consultant on Program Services

National Association for Retarded Citizens

University Park Press
Baltimore

UNIVERSITY PARK PRESS
International Publishers in Science, Medicine, and Education
233 East Redwood Street
Baltimore, Maryland 21202

Copyright © 1980 by University Park Press

Typeset by Action Comp. Co., Inc.
Manufactured in the United States of America by
The Maple Press Company.

Library of Congress Cataloging in Publication Data
Main entry under title:
Shaping the future.
"Based on a national conference held December 4–5, 1978 in Phoenix,
Arizona . . . planned and sponsored by the National Association for
Retarded Citizens (NARC) Research and Demonstration Institute and
NARC's national Residential Services and Facilities Committee."
Bibliography: p.
Includes index.
1. Mentally handicapped—Services for—United States—Congresses.
I. Roos, Philip. II. McCann, Brian M. III. Addison, Max R. IV. National
Association for Retarded Citizens Research and Demonstration Institute.
V. National Association for Retarded Citizens Residential Services and
Facilities Committee.
HV3006.A4S63   362.3   79-23618
ISBN 0-8391-1547-4

CONTENTS

CONTRIBUTORS

Max R. Addison, M.S.
Consultant on Program Services
National Association for Retarded
  Citizens Research and Demon-
  stration Institute
P.O. Box 6109
Arlington, Texas 76011

Thomas K. Gilhool, M.A., L.L.B.
Chief Counsel
Public Interest Law Center of
  Philadelphia
1315 Walnut Street, 16th Floor
Philadelphia, Pennsylvania 19107

Jennifer L. Howse, Ph.D.
Associate Commissioner of Mental
  Retardation and Developmental
  Disabilities for New York City
  and Long Island
2 World Trade Center
Room 5657
New York, New York 10047

Andrea S. Knight
Board Member, National Association
  for Retarded Citizens
573 Longwood Avenue
Glencoe, Illinois 60022

Frank Laski
Director, Advocacy Training
Developmental Disabilities Center
Temple University, and
Staff Attorney
Public Interest Law Center of
  Philadelphia
1315 Walnut Street, 16th Floor
Philadelphia, Pennsylvania 19107

Brian R. Lensink
Assistant Director
Division of Developmental Disabilities
  and Mental Retardation Services
Department of Economic Security
P.O. Box 6760
Phoenix, Arizona 85005

Brian M. McCann, Ph.D.
Institute Director
National Association for Retarded
  Citizens Research and Demonstra-
  tion Institute
P.O. Box 6109
Arlington, Texas 76011

Gene Patterson, R.N., F.A.A.M.D.
Executive Director
Association for Retarded Citizens
  of Fort Worth
1300 West Lancaster
Fort Worth, Texas 76102

Philip Roos, Ph.D.
Executive Director
National Association for Retarded
  Citizens
P.O. Box 6109
Arlington, Texas 76011

Richard C. Scheerenberger, Ph.D.
Superintendent
Central Wisconsin Center for the
  Developmentally Disabled
317 Knutson Drive
Madison, Wisconsin 53704

Charles J. Seevers, Ph.D.
Executive Director
Association for the Disabled of
 Elkhart County, Inc.
Aux Chandelles
P.O. Box 398
Bristol, Indiana 46507

Louis M. Thrasher, J.D.
Special Counsel for Litigation
Civil Rights Division
Room 5712
U.S. Department of Justice
Washington, D.C. 20530

James R. Wilson, Jr., M.B.A.
President
National Association for Retarded
 Citizens
45 Rockefeller Plaza
New York, New York 10020

FOREWORD

In October, 1963, during the National Association for Retarded Citizens' annual convention in Washington, D.C., President John F. Kennedy signed into law the Retardation Planning Amendment. This important piece of legislation set into motion planning activities across the nation to establish community systems to serve mentally retarded persons. Each state's plans were unique according to their needs.

Other federal legislation was to follow, including amendments to the Social Security Act, Medicaid, the Developmental Disabilities Act, the Rehabilitation Act of 1973, particularly Section 504, and the Education for All Handicapped Children Act of 1975, which would allow states to change and expand their plans as more was learned about providing effective services.

The availability of funds influenced the direction of these changes and brought into focus issues surrounding the living environments of retarded people.

The Symposium on Nursing Homes, held by the National Association for Retarded Citizens (NARC) in Chicago in 1974, responded to the transfer of retarded persons, often inappropriately, from public institutions into skilled nursing homes (SNFs) and Intermediate Care Facilities (ICFs). The proceedings included a position statement adopted by NARC on the use of nursing homes to serve retarded persons. Two years later NARC held a National Forum on Residential Services in New Orleans in 1976, which provided a showcase of four types of residential services: the institution, the village, the community living arrangement, and foster family living. This forum made available basic information for developing and implementing a comprehensive system of residential services.

As was clearly indicated at these major national conferences, the principles of normalization, least restrictive alternative, and integration are now well documented and accepted by the professional community. Yet many bureaucratic planners continue to draft designs for self-contained, segregated "centers" for people who are developmentally disabled. They still propose the use of vacated buildings on the grounds of hospitals for mentally ill or tubercular patients or the remodeling of underutilized general hospitals. Once again, consumer groups are protesting the inappropriate placement of mentally retarded persons in nursing homes.

Advocates for retarded people have redoubled their efforts to establish small, community-based residential services. Resistance to these community-based alternatives has been bolstered by scandals surrounding the irresponsible abandonment of mentally ill persons in communities, despite the obvious difference between mentally ill and mentally retarded persons. State and local officials have cried "no money," while federal and state agencies commit millions of dollars to residential facilities that keep people who are retarded isolated, segregated, and in unnecessarily restrictive environments.

Where traditional methods of negotiation and persuasion have failed, several Associations for Retarded Citizens have taken, or are considering taking, departments of state government to court, seeking remedies to injustices and inequities resulting from inappropriate settings for retarded people.

Shaping the Future presents the underlying principles and the components of an adequate, integrated community service system which includes residential services; identifies obstacles to its development and the value issues behind them; emphasizes the necessity of posing the proper questions and recommendations to the court when litigation is necessary; and discusses methods and strategies for implementing a favorable court order. The results of court action and the enacting of legislation to implement court orders will have impact on the future for retarded people. The importance of careful planning and consideration of possible results before seeking the intervention of the courts becomes obvious.

Eleanor S. Elkin
Past President NARC

PREFACE

This book is based on a national conference held December 4–5, 1978, in Phoenix, Arizona. The meeting was planned and sponsored by the National Association for Retarded Citizens (NARC) Research and Demonstration Institute and the NARC Residential Services and Facilities Committee.

The contents of this book represent an initial attempt to compile information about the processes and methods currently being used for establishing community-based facilities and services for mentally retarded people. A movement away from outmoded and inappropriate service approaches and concepts toward community-based programs and services is described by those who are primarily involved in the transition (i.e., representatives from the fields of education, psychology, law, and government).

Since the information presented by the various authorities represents divergent fields of interest as well as differing viewpoints, the reader will note that there is no consensus among the authors concerning the assignment of priorities for specific concepts or activities relative to establishing community-based services. The newness of the service approaches described makes disagreement of this nature unavoidable. The interchange generated by such conflicting opinions should further the development of efficient service delivery systems for retarded citizens through cooperative efforts to provide effective community-based services.

It is hoped that the information presented will help service providers, parents, and advocates develop a full understanding of the new philosophies and goals that underlie the emerging service approach for meeting the individual needs of mentally retarded people.

SHAPING
THE
FUTURE

1
SOME NECESSARY CONDITIONS FOR A COMMUNITY SERVICES SYSTEM

Thomas K. Gilhool

In his study for the President's Committee on Mental Retardation, the first chapter of the latest revised edition of *Changing Patterns in Residential Services for the Mentally Retarded* (1976), Earl Butterfield ranked Illinois, Connecticut, Michigan, and Pennsylvania highest among the states in efforts to provide decent institutional care. On the basis of his look at all the states in the union, Butterfield concluded:

> If it were shown that these states—Pennsylvania, Michigan, Connecticut, Illinois—provide inadequate care in their institutions, then there truly would be reason to seek completely different treatment alternatives for this nation's mentally retarded people (p. 34).

Yet Judge Broderick has found the care in Pennsylvania's Pennhurst State School inadequate (*Halderman* v. *Pennhurst State School and Hospital*, 446 F. Supp. 1295 (E.D. Pa. 1977)); Judge Joiner has found the care in Michigan's Plymouth State School inadequate (*Michigan Association for Retarded Citizens* v. *Smith*, C.A. No. 78-70384, Preliminary Injunction of March 3, 1978); and the Connecticut Association for Retarded Citizens filed a lawsuit seeking to replace Mansfield Training Center and the nursing homes that Mansfield provides with community services (*Connecticut Association for Retarded Citizens, Inc.* v. *Mansfield Training School,* C.A. No. 78-653, Complaint of December 8, 1978).

Judge Broderick, at the initiative of the Pennsylvania Association for Retarded Citizens, and based on the record of a 9-week trial, found the Pennhurst school to represent a monumental example of unconstitutionality. He found that the facility did not provide, nor could it provide, adequate services to retarded people. Yet Pennhurst was not, and is not, the worst of Pennsylvania's institutions. The school has one of the highest staff ratios in the country; it has very little staff turnover; and expenditures at Pennhurst are $26,000 per person annually.

The 1,200 people residing at Pennhurst are typical of the nearly 200,000 residents in public institutions across the country. On the average, the residents of Pennhurst are 35 years old, have resided there 21 years, and were admitted when they were children; most (74%) are severely or profoundly retarded.

At the initiative of the Michigan Association for Retarded Citizens, Judge Joiner needed only 2 hours to determine that at the Plymouth institution conditions were such that it was necessary for him to issue immediate, emergency relief. Plymouth is one of Michigan's newest facilities. Three-fourths of the population is of school age (in Michigan, defined as under 25 years old) and, therefore, leaves the institution for about 5½–6 hours a day to attend what is, by all reports, an excellent school system. Yet care at the institution has been declared inadequate.

The judicial findings are clear: three of the four states that Butterfield identified as having tried the hardest to serve the mentally handicapped population have failed. There is good reason indeed to seek a completely different service system for retarded people.

In this chapter some of the conditions necessary for the systematic replacement of institutions with systems of community services are discussed. Four particular issues must be addressed and resolved if effective, reliable, continuing systems of community services are to be created: 1) funding, 2) the allocation of responsibility for creating monitoring and accountability mechanisms, 3) finding jobs for institution employees, and 4) assessing the retardation movement itself, in particular the attention that must be given to the dilemmas faced by institutional parents, dilemmas that must be addressed if a system of community services is to be created to replace institutions.

With respect to each of the four, testimony of three witnesses in the Pennhurst case is especially relevant: Elsie Schmidt, then President of the Pennsylvania Association for Retarded Citizens and now Regional Vice-President of the National Association for Retarded Citizens (NARC); Stewart Brown, then the immediate past President of the Pennsylvania Association for Retarded Citizens; and Gunnar Dybwad, currently President of the International League of Societies for the Mentally Handicapped. The discussion that follows also borrows liberally from Teddi Leiden, the current President of the Pennsylvania Association for Retarded Citizens.

THE PROBLEM OF FUNDING

Howse addresses the funding dilemmas of Title XIX of the Social Security Act of 1971 in Chapter 5. No single factor contributes more to the perpetuation and continuation of the institutional system than the current implementation of Title XIX. The result has been encouragement to the states to continue the institutions rather than to replace them. There is a great irony to this because Congress, in amending the Social Security Act in 1971 to allow Title XIX funds for Intermediate Care Facilities for the Mentally Retarded (ICF/MRs), apparently had no such intention.

The same Congress that opened Title XIX funds to ICF/MRs also, in the same act, adopted, amended, and created such mechanisms as "independent professional review" and "periodic on-site inspections prior to admission review" in all intermediate care facilities to determine the necessity and desirability of continued placement in such facilities and the feasibility of meeting needs through alternative services (42 U.S.C. 1396(a)(31)). The purpose of these mechanisms, the Congress said, was "to assure...that each [person] is in the right place at the right time receiving the right care" (117 Cong. Rec. 44721 (December 4, 1971)).

Furthermore, Congress's purpose in adding ICF/MRs to Title XIX was clear. It was to contribute federal funds to underwrite: "The active provision of *rehabilitative, educational* and *training services* to enhance that capacity of mentally retarded individuals to care for themselves or to engage in employment" (117 Cong. Rec. 44720 (December 4, 1971)). Congress did not regard ICF/MRs as expressions of the medical model. Rather, it explicitly saw the services it was underwriting in the ICF/MR provision as "rehabilitative, educational and training services."

By and large, of course, the opposite has happened, and Title XIX funds have thus far, with some notable exceptions, flowed exclusively to the large medical-model institutions. That flow of federal funds has, for more than a decade, undergirded and sustained institutions long past their time, despite a widespread realization that large, central institutions are not the place-of-choice for services to retarded people. The flow of institution-sustaining funds has inhibited and slowed the creation of alternative community-based services for retarded people. Congressional members did not contemplate and did not intend the consequences that have ensued. It was not their intention that they should underwrite medical-model institutional non-services. It was rather their intention, in the 1971 amendments, to encourage and to underwrite non-medical-model, effective services of the rehabilitative, educational, and training sort for retarded people.

One current pressing question is whether the Title XIX funding stream can be put back on track, on the track Congress intended—in particular, whether Title XIX can be made to flow in meaningful amounts to support small-scale, community-based facilities and services, including specifically the so-called "ICF/MRs under 16." The statute and the regulations so allow. (Indeed, the congressional purpose would seem to so command.) The ICF/MR regulations state:

> For purpose of Federal financial participation ... "Institution" means an establishment which furnishes (in single *or* multiple facilities) food and shelter to four or more persons unrelated to the proprietor and in addition, provides some treatment or services which meet some need beyond the basic provision of food and shelter (45 C.F.R. 448.60(b)(1)).

Difficulties as well as successes have been experienced in New York, Minnesota, Michigan, Oklahoma, and Massachusetts in transmuting Title XIX funds from an institution-sustaining funding stream to one that will foster and support community services. But results in these states confirm that it can be done. The clearest, and the primary, recommendation of the U.S. Department of Health, Education, and Welfare's (HEW) Deinstitutionalization Task Force was that the Secretary should instruct the Health Care Facilities Administration (HCFA) and the HEW regional offices to use Title XIX ICF/MR under 16 funds to create and sustain services in the community without the constraint of the medical model. To date, these recommendations, which were endorsed unanimously by the state commissioners' subgroup of the Deinstitutionalization Task Force (composed of state mental health/mental retardation directors), have not yet been acted upon. If the Secretary of HEW does not respond to these recommendations, Congress may have to.

The problem raised by Title XIX, standing as it now does as a major inhibition to the replacement of institutions by systems of community services, is a matter that must be addressed in the course of the next few years by all constituencies concerned with services for retarded people and, indeed, by constituencies for all disabled people. A national strategy can yield, in the course of the next few years, a congressional charter for long-term community-based services and an untrammeled funding stream for long-term community-based services.

Consider what was experienced in the early 1970s. After *Pennsylvania Association for Retarded Children (PARC)* v. *Commonwealth of Pennsylvania*, 343 F. Supp. 279 (E.D. Pa. 1972), declared the right to equal educational opportunity, and as cases in courts in Washington, D.C., New Orleans, Michigan, and elsewhere across the country did the same, Senators Humphrey, Williams, Stafford, and Matthias, Congressman Bradamus, and a host of others took up the equal protection theme. They proceeded to write the court orders and declarations of the right to education into the law of the land. These were effective first in the 1974 Education Amendments and then in the 1975 Education for All Handicapped Children Act, P.L. 94-142. The right to education was thus ensured in each of the 50 states by act of Congress.

The judicial force of community services cases already decided, and to be decided within the next few months, makes possible congressional application of the same equal protection theme to residential services. Congress, unlike a court, by its legislative power can make that theme sound across the country and can redesign funding streams, as is necessary, so that full systems of community services can become a reality.

Judge Bartels, who succeeded to the Willowbrook case (*New York State Association for Retarded Children, Inc.* v. *Carey*, 393 F. Supp. 715 (E.D.N.Y. 1975)) after the death of Judge Judd, has made some important recent decisions. The residual anticipated by the original Willowbrook orders, namely, an institution with 250 people, is no longer contemplated. This change in posture by the court is the result of several considerations. Efforts to improve Willowbrook have been futile. It has become obvious that no retarded person requires such a large-scale and segregated environment as Willowbrook in order to receive effective services. It has also become clear that Congress has made the judgment that adequate services must be provided for all in the most integrated setting possible. Judge Bartels, in contested proceeding, has made it clear that the Willowbrook case requires the creation of community services for *all* retarded people heretofore at Willowbrook. In his Opinion of June 10, 1977, Judge Bartels wrote:

> The goals of normalization and development of the mentally retarded cannot be met until every effort is made to physically and socially integrate the class members into the mainstream of the community. . . . The services delivered to them should be in the same context as community services delivered to others. . . .
>
> It is in community placement where the only real improvement in the handicapped and retarded can be expected (*NYSARC* v. *Carey*, C.A. No. 72-C-357, Opinion of June 10, 1977, at 11-12).

In his Opinion of September 14, 1978, Judge Bartels wrote:

> The most serious consequences of the Board's plan would be felt if the pupils were sent to school in developmental centers. The court is convinced that this would have a severely retrogressive effect on the development of these children, and would be an enormous setback to the process of normalization of these children. . . .
>
> The argument of the Board that because the Track IV children have little contact with normal children in the public schools, they would not be harmed by the complete absence of such contact in development center schools must be entirely rejected. Association with normal persons is the primary means by which mentally retarded persons improve and develop, and its importance cannot be overestimated. Conversely, retarded persons who associate primarily with other retarded persons generally adopt retrogressive behavior patterns

and will usually deteriorate. It is for this reason that the Staten Island Developmental Center (Willowbrook) is being ordered emptied (*NYSARC* v. *Carey*, C.A. No. 72-C-357 E.D.N.Y., Opinion of September 14, 1978, at 14-15).

Judge Broderick has expressed a similar sentiment in the *Pennhurst* case. Having found that "... the confinement and isolation of the retarded in the institution called Pennhurst is segregation in a facility that clearly is separate and *not* equal," (446 F. Supp. 1295, 1231-32 (E.D. Pa. 1977)), Judge Broderick wrote:

> The retarded at Pennhurst are not receiving minimally adequate habilitation and...such habilitation cannot be provided at Pennhurst because it does not provide an atmosphere conducive to normalization. ...
> Great caution and care must be exercised to make certain that each and every retarded resident who is moved from Pennhurst can be accommodated in a community facility which *will* provide minimally adequate habilitation... (446 F. Supp. at 1325).

He further ordered:

> Commonwealth and county defendants are enjoined to provide suitable community living arrangements for the retarded residents at Pennhurst and those retarded persons on the waiting list, together with such community services as are necessary to provide them with minimally adequate habilitation ... (446 F. Supp. at 1326).

Judge Pratt of the Federal District Court in Washington, D.C., has approved a consent decree to the same effect, requiring that the institution at Forest Haven be fully replaced by a system of community services (*Evans* v. *Washington*, C.A. No. 76-0293, Judgment and Order of June 14, 1978). Likewise, Judge Boyle of the Federal District Court in Rhode Island has approved a consent decree setting in motion three plans to replace Rhode Island's institutions with a system of community services (*Isamone* v. *Garrahy*, C.A. No. 77-0727, Order of April 6, 1979).

The Kentucky Association for Retarded Citizens is halfway through trial in their efforts to secure a similar judgment. They are attempting to prevent the building of a new institution called Outwood, and instead seek the creation of community services of sufficient quality and quantity so that Outwood will be unnecessary. Many other Associations for Retarded Citizens are also in court seeking similar orders to create community services to replace institutions. Such actions are underway in New Hampshire, Florida, Texas, Colorado, and Washington.

There is nothing automatic, of course, about the translation of injunctions and imperatives into further statutory enactment by Congress, but it has happened often in the last 30 years in many matters concerning the civil rights of Americans. Other trends suggest that Congress must, in any event, grapple with the Title XIX system within the next few years.

Congress is acutely conscious of the cost explosion under Title XIX. If only for that reason, congressional members must address the issue. This should provide the opportunity to obtain a nationally legislated charter for community services that clearly delineates a non-medical model, supported by a community-based funding stream that can provide long-term services for retarded people.

It is the author's opinion that the retardation movement can approach such an effort most effectively through close association with other handicapped populations and their advocates. The question of long-term community-based services is as relevant to physically disabled, elderly, and mentally ill persons as it is to retarded persons. In an effort toward this direction, the Rehabilitation Act of 1978, for the first time, includes a section called Comprehensive Services for Independent Living (Title VII). This legislation is important to the retarded, the physically disabled, the elderly, and the severely mentally ill. All share a common concern for the appropriateness and effectiveness of residential services. All are interested in small-scale, comunity-based, effective services and in securing a congressional charter ensuring a clear funding stream for these services.

IMPLEMENTING MONITORING AND ACCOUNTABILITY MECHANISMS

Another vital question relates to the issue of responsibility. It is essential to create, design, and put in place structures that allocate clear responsibility for providing community services that include monitoring and accountability mechanisms. That services of the necessary quantity and quality will be provided on an ongoing and coordinated basis must be ensured.

Much has been learned from experience with mechanisms to regulate nursing homes and boarding homes, as well as from monitoring and establishing systems of accountability for the education of handicapped children. The Massachusetts special education experience provides an example of an effective approach to monitoring and accountability. For example, a set of intensive and well-focused *regulatory mechanisms* like those in force in Massachusetts are necessary. These include: 1) site visitation on a regular basis by professionals and consumers who have been trained to identify problems and to develop a plan of correction, 2) an intriguing and effective system (based upon periodic surveys of teachers and other personnel) for measuring the continuing needs of those who work in the schools and for providing continuing inservice education, and 3) a system of sanctions to enforce standards. Such regulatory mechanisms are only one dimension of an effective monitoring system.

Another important approach, which focuses on *programming*, is illustrated in such states as Minnesota and California. These states have developed mechanisms and procedures for measuring the progress of retarded people in the attainment of skills. The measures also provide the basis for evaluating the performance of the service system and for discovering specific problems.

A third dimension of the responsibility, monitoring, and accountability system relates to mechanisms of *inspection and enforcement*. Experience with attempts to regulate nursing homes has provided much information on how these mechanisms can be improved.

It is clear that regulating, licensing, inspecting, monitoring, and enforcing cannot be totally accomplished from a distance. The 50-year history of the regulation of corporations in this country, richly reviewed by Christopher Stone in *Where the Law Ends* (1975), illustrates that much can be done by monitoring and regulating at a distance but that it is necessary to have up-close mechanisms as well. That is, effective monitoring requires mechanisms that are part of, or closely related to, the system being monitored. There are a host of such mechanisms with a history of effectiveness. These include, for example, the requirement that each community service provider have a board consisting of persons representing a broad spectrum of interests, including representatives from Associations for Retarded Citizens (ARCs), United Cerebral Palsy Associations (UCPs), and the Epilepsy Foundation of America (EFA). Such members are needed because of their organizational experience and knowledge of service problems and issues.

Another effective mechanism is the friend/advocate system. This approach has many advantages; it can meet numerous personal needs of retarded people as well as provide an effective tool for monitoring and enforcing. This one-to-one advocacy by knowledgeable and observant people in community-living programs provides the opportunity for early detection of problems and efforts to secure corrections. Such a network of one-to-one friends/advocates undoubtedly must be sustained and supported by an additional network of specialized advocates. These specialists characteristically come from the staffs and committees of the voluntary organizations, such as the ARCs, and UCPs, and EFA. They are sophisticated in the areas as education, vocational rehabilitation, employment, recreation, and so on.

THE ISSUE OF EMPLOYMENT

The second greatest obstacle to the replacement of institutions by a system of community services is federal, state, and local governments' failure to ensure that the people presently employed by the institutions have future employment possibilities. There are 1,500 employees and 1,200 residents at Pennhurst. For the nearly 100,000 mentally retarded people in public retardation institutions in the country, there are almost as many employees. These employees deserve serious consideration. The political facts of life require addressing their employment needs. In a society where work is central to our way of life and where employment is often scarce and difficult to obtain, the economic needs of these workers must be addressed on their own merits as a matter of justice. Thus, developing equitable arrangements for the employment of the institutions' current employees is a necessary condition to creating a system of community services.

THE ROLE OF PARENTS WITHIN THE RETARDATION MOVEMENT

Another necessary ingredient in successful transition to community-based residential services is best exemplified by the testimony of 77-year-old Grace Auerbach, an immigrant at the age of 9 from Russia to the United States. Her son, Sidney, entered Pennhurst in the mid-1930s. He left Pennhurst about 1975, and has since lived first in a group home and now in a supervised apartment with two retarded friends. According to his mother, while at Pennhurst Sidney was subdued and never talked; now he is always ready to engage in conversation. He is employed and has his own bank account. Sidney has learned more in the last 3½ years while in the community than he did in the 38 years that he resided at Pennhurst. After a carefully structured living experience, he is able to travel to work by bus, making two changes. He invites his mother regularly to breakfast on Sunday, and, in his mother's words, "He looks like a million dollars." Sidney Auerbach is severely retarded. Mrs. Auerbach testified that for 1½ years after the staff at Pennhurst had suggested moving to a community-living arrangement she felt it was impossible and refused to allow the move. She did not believe he could be self-sufficient after all the years at Pennhurst, certainly not as severely retarded as he was. Yet, she finally made the decision, and all of her testimony to the court emphasized that she was pleased with the decision.

Judge Broderick found that often people are in institutions not because others wanted to put them there, but because those who cared for them at the time they entered the institution had no choices available. The fact that so many parents took this action years ago has enormous consequences and important dimensions for today's efforts toward deinstitutionalization. The investment accompanying a decision made with difficulty and with great travail is not to be taken lightly. Parents do not want to hear that they made a wrong decision, and it is small consolation to be told it was a right decision in 1956 because of the conditions at the time but that now conditions have changed and the right decision is community placement. How can parents be assured that community services will be ongoing and will be of the requisite quality? Parents say "show me." It is a necessary condition of the systematic implementation of community services that each of the necessary conditions discussed above, such as appropriate monitoring, accountability, and responsibility systems, and a stable funding stream, be present. Only the fulfillment of these conditions will ultimately satisfy the "show me" demands of institutional parents.

Parents who committed their children to institutions approximately 21 years ago when their children were an average of 13 years old did so when no community alternatives existed. Coping with that decision and the chronic brutality that followed has enormous consequences for every parent: some have withdrawn; some have embraced the institution and will adamantly defend it and their original decision; others, those in the Associations for Retarded Citizens and other volunteer organizations, have worked long and hard to create alternatives so that other parents will not have to face such decisions. That work must soon come to completion.

REFERENCES

Butterfield, E. 1976. Some basic changes in residential facilities. In: R. Kugel and A. Shearer (eds.), Changing Patterns in Residential Services for the Mentally Retarded, pp. 15, 33–34. Rev. ed. President's Committee on Mental Retardation, Washington, D.C.
Stone, C. 1975. Where the Law Ends: The Social Control of Corporate Behavior. Harper & Row, New York.

2

DEALING WITH THE MOMENTUM OF OUTMODED APPROACHES

Philip Roos

According to a contemporary theory, people choose when to die. This decision is usually made when the future generates so much anxiety that continued existence is no longer meaningful. In this day of rapid change, most people do experience the future as a source of confusion and anxiety.

Anxiety has been defined in many different ways, but Fritz Perls' (1973) definition is particularly relevant to this discussion. Perls, the father of Gestalt psychotherapy, defined anxiety as the gap between the now and the later. As soon as an individual leaves the secure status of the now and projects himself into the future, he is likely to experience anxiety.

When considering resistance to change, anxiety is therefore a focal concept. Using Perls' framework, it is evident that one can decide to become anxious merely by thinking about the future—not the present, because most people feel reasonably comfortable at any given moment—and not the past, because that is done and finished. But if a person dwells on anticipated catastrophes that lie ahead—the death of a family member, illness, departure of one's children, the loss of a job, and so forth—he generates his own anxiety. These types of anticipations are sources of anxiety not only for individuals but for organizations as well. Most people have developed great skill in minimizing such anxiety, and organizations have evolved similar mechanisms. To deal effectively with the momentum of outmoded approaches requires, therefore, an understanding of defenses against the anxiety of change.

DEFENSES AGAINST CHANGE

A typical tactic used by individuals and organizations to minimize anxiety is *denial*, the refusal to recognize the reality of possible change. This approach is epitomized by the old saying, "There is nothing new under the sun." Likewise, the French have a beautiful saying, "The more things change, the more they stay the same." In the field of mental retardation, this attitude is reflected in such statements as, "There will always be institutions," and "There will always be people who are so handicapped that they will need institutions."

Another defense against change is *traditionalism*—clinging to the past and appealing to history and past authorities as justification for maintaining the status quo. A superb example can be found in the field of education. It has been known for decades that didactic education, such as that exemplified by the proceedings of most national conferences where one professional presents his views to his colleagues, is probably the least effective of all approaches to education. Yet most universities and schools continue to use this ineffective model.

The concept of *functional autonomy*, advanced by psychologist Gordon Allport (1937), is yet another defense against change. This theory holds that motives may become independent of their origins and continue to operate even though they are no longer functional. Thus organizations sanctify procedures and policies. Systems become self-sustaining. An anecdote recounted by Bill Sloan (personal communication), former superintendent of the Austin State School, can serve as an example. While superintendent of another institution, he one day questioned the daily sounding of the laundry whistle at 10:30 a.m.: "Why does that blooming whistle blow? Nothing happens. Nobody goes to eat. There is no shift change." His devoted staff traced down the enigmatic practice and found that many years before there had been a shift change at that time. Although this shift change had long since been abandoned, the whistle blowing had become functionally autonomous.

Futurists have also labeled *discounting* as another defense against change. This mechanism refers to the tendency to dwell in the present and be concerned with immediate crises, while discounting the distant future and the distant past. An example is the problem faced by professionals trying to deal with the energy crisis. It is extremely difficult to generate interest in what is anticipated 10 years from now. But if people are told of an impending gasoline shortage next week, they become highly excited. Those who are familiar with the mode of operation of boards of directors can probably attest that a great deal of time is spent dealing with current problems compared with planning, even if only for 2 years hence.

Finally, the defense of *supersimplification* consists of seeking unitary solutions for highly complex problems (Toffler, 1970). In the field of mental retardation, such concepts as "normalization," "developmental programming," and "deinstitutionalization" have sometimes been embraced as *the* answer to all anticipated problems and unresolved issues.

These general defenses against the anxiety of change have become prevalent in the field of mental retardation, a field undergoing major changes and revolutionary upheavals in philosophy and ideology. The principal concepts underlying these changes include normalization, the developmental mode, individualization, and self-enhancement or self-actualization (Roos, 1972; Roos, 1979; Roos and McCann, 1977). Each of these concepts has generated controversy, anxiety, and defensiveness.

RESISTANCE TO DEINSTITUTIONALIZATION

Defenses against change have certainly been erected in response to the proposed abandonment of large multipurpose institutions. Elsewhere in this volume (Chapters 8 and 11), allusion is made to the fact that so-called deinstitutionalization is proceeding haphazardly and, in many cases, without the least success. The following discussion explores some of the reasons for the pervasive reluctance to abandon a model that is so widely recognized as an anachronism.

Some of the problems are easily traced to organizational inertia. Any large, complex organization develops considerable inertia, which results in serious obstacles to change. These include problems inherent in bureaucracy, such as policies, procedures, budget restraints, and regulations. Often, changing any of these elements requires the approval of a multitude of people, which may include legislators and other elected officials.

A different class of problems often can be attributed to the administrators of such complex systems (Roos, 1969). Administrators, if they have any tenure at all, have mastered self-protective tactics. Often they have learned that they are more likely to be fired for sins of commission than for sins of omission. Doing nothing is often the preferred approach of the seasoned administrator. He recognizes that the typical organization is in a highly tenuous homeostatic balance, and that if change is introduced at any point the whole system is likely to crumble and disintegrate. Hence, implementing any change is potentially hazardous to the administrator.

Changing complex systems is usually complicated because it involves a number of separate subcultures. At least three distinct subcultures have been identified as typical of large state institutions (Roos, 1970). Each subculture has its own values and norms which, not infrequently, may be mutually inconsistent. Thus, changes sanctioned by one group may be actively opposed by another.

Another source of resistance to change involves management rationales that have been advanced for retaining the institution in its current form. These include the following:

It would be economically unsound to sacrifice the existing capital investment typically committed to large facilities—the big buildings, the land, the renovations, and so forth.

The cost-benefit data comparing institutions with community-based residential programs are still unclear and inconsistent.

The funding streams currently available tend to favor institutions. Indeed, some of the federal programs serve as disincentives to deinstitutionalization. Howse (Chapter 5) has described with great skill and imagination how one can combine various federal funding streams and orchestrate them into mechanisms to fund community programs. The process is highly complex and fluid, however, so that only the most sophisticated administrator is enthusiastic about orchestrating the elusive resources.

Another major problem is the relative inaccessibility of services in community settings. The National Association for Retarded Citizens (1977) recently conducted a survey that documents the kinds of problems often experienced in trying to access the generic services.

Concern has also been expressed that community settings may lead to ineffective and inefficient deployment of resources. Thus, it is argued by some that a large group of profoundly or severely retarded people must be concentrated in a single location to warrant provision of the necessary professional, specialized expertise they need. That is, a critical mass of clients is essential to justify the necessary services.

Since many administrators prefer management through control rather than management through persuasion, decentralized community models provide an uncomfortable situation.

Finally, administrators contend that it is much more difficult to clearly identify the foci of responsibility and accountability in a dispersed system than it is in a traditional, centralized model, such as the typical institution.

A different type of rationale is colloquially referred to as the PTA rationale, that is, the protect the gluteus rationale. Economic and political arguments dominate this approach. Institutions are pollution-free industries, and the threat of losing such a source of local revenue is likely to generate strong political and economic opposition. Another manifestation of this syndrome is concern for maintenance of job security and the fears of institutional staff that decentralization will mean either retraining, which is disgraceful enough, or being phased out, which may be even more disastrous. The unions, of course, often enter into this situation to "protect" institutional employees. Finally, many institutions have been supported by voluntary auxiliary bodies. Most skilled superintendents nurture outside groups who become their personal advocates as well as supporters of the institution. Examples include volunteer councils and parent-type organizations.

A new rationale that has recently surfaced can be dubbed the "incompetence model." It is being advanced by some scientists and professionals. Its basic premise is that some mentally retarded people lack the capacity to benefit from formal programming and that, consequently, they should not be involved in systematic training programs. A specific example can be found in the recent *Motion for Modification* by defendants in the Partlow, Alabama, case (*Wyatt* v. *Aderholt*), 368 F. Supp. 1382 (M.D. Ala. 1973), enforced 368 F. Supp. 1383 (1974), *sub nom. Wyatt* v. *Hardin,* Motion for Modification, pp. 4, 8, 23 (1978). It appears that a number of "national experts in mental retardation" have proposed that the court decree, which was based on the concept of the right to treatment, be significantly modified. Their conclusion is based on their claim that many retarded people lack the capacity to benefit from programming. They argue that

> ... the behavior of many (Partlow residents) cannot reasonably be expected to improve significantly with training, even for living within the sheltered environment of an institution. ... Only a minority ... are likely to acquire even basic self-help skills in training which improve their daily lives and which they will continue to use on a daily basis after the 'training' is discontinued (*Wyatt* v. *Aderholt*, Motion for Modification, 1978).

Furthermore, this position argues that some mentally retarded people plateau early and that additional training is useless. Thus, with regard to Partlow, these "experts" claim that after more than 6 years of intensive training activity, no significant progress has been made with many residents: "... to pursue a daily regimen of training with those who are not profiting from such training, and who may not be participating in the activity by choice, is punishing and demeaning" (*Wyatt* v. *Aderholt*, Motion for Modification, 1978). They conclude that "to require a human being to participate involuntarily in a futile daily training regimen extending over months, even years, may constitute cruel and inhuman treatment" (*Wyatt* v. *Aderholt*, Motion for Modification, 1978). Furthermore, it is claimed by those who endorse the incompetence model that institutions may provide a legitimate, essentially custodial—rather than training or habilitation—function.

Another rationale is based on what might be called the *security model*. According to this point of view, severely retarded people should be protected from society, where they are likely to be exploited. It is argued, for example, that there is a relatively high incidence of mental retardation in the criminal justice system. Proponents of this view claim that increased risk is associated with community placement, and some statistical and research evidence can be marshalled to support this position (Nihira and Nihira, 1975).

Yet another rationale is based on what has been called the *hedonistic model* (Roos, 1979), that is, the concept that the primary objective in programming for retarded people is to foster their happiness and contentment. Proponents of this position argue that within the institution even the severely retarded individual is part of a community where he has a meaningful role, and where he finds love and acceptance. On the other hand, if he were living in the community, he would be at the bottom of the socioeconomic ladder, unable to compete with others and without status or recognition. He would be a "loser" instead of a "winner."

In addition, a number of rationales are founded on parental anxieties and concerns. These parental feelings cannot be dismissed as mere manifestations of overprotectiveness or emotionalism. It is important to recognize that there are parents who strongly resist deinstitutionalization, and that some of their reasons may be based on realistic considerations. Some of their major concerns include the following:

Parents question the security of funding and fear that community programs are likely to be tenuous and transitory. Shifting funding patterns and fluidity of administrative models tend to reinforce these concerns.

Loci of responsibility and accountability are often vague and confusing in community-based residential systems, in contrast with the clearly structured management of the typical institution. Hence, parents may not know to whom to turn when they wish to question or challenge the system.

Some parents are anxious about the health and safety of their child in community facilities. They feel that some of these settings present greater risks than the relatively self-contained institution, and they may be unwilling to accept the threat of increased dangers in exchange for potentially greater freedom.

Other parents fear that deinstitutionalization will ultimately result in having their child returned to them, and they may feel unable and/or unwilling to cope with this possibility. They may, for example, recall the catastrophic situations that led to institutionalization in the first place, or their child may be an adult and placement in the home may no longer be appropriate. Thus, many parents of both normal and handicapped children feel that the normative pattern in contemporary society is for parental emancipation from their children once they have reached adulthood.

Anxiety is particularly likely to surface when parent surrogates, such as foster parents, are selected as the approach to deinstitutionalization. Parents may feel threatened that these "strangers" will be more successful than they themselves were, confirming their own feelings of failure and challenging their original decision to institutionalize their child.

Finally, some parents are fearful of reactivating old conflicts that they painfully resolved when they originally placed their child in an institution. Typically, the decision was extremely painful and accompanied by guilt and grief. Understandably, the parents do not wish to re-experience these past traumas, nor do they wish to face the possibility that their past decisions may not have been in their child's best interest.

OVERCOMING OBSTACLES TO CHANGE

In developing approaches to overcome these obstacles, it is useful to adopt the principle that one is more likely to be successful using carrots than sticks. Or, in behavioral terms, applying positive reinforcement is more effective than inflicting punishment. Change could acquire positive rather than negative connotations. Ideally, people will change because they want to change, and because the anticipated conditions are more desirable than the current ones. It is important, therefore, to emphasize that proposed changes will increase rather than decrease options for choice, so that the consumer will have greater rather than less freedom. Thus, it becomes essential to provide a wide selection of desirable alternatives.

Another approach to overcoming resistance to change is to establish and to disseminate models of effective approaches to change. Thus, prototypes are needed to demonstrate ways of bringing about change in different settings. These models should not only illustrate practical and effective methods for implementing change, but they should also emphasize the desirable consequences of change.

It is also necessary to modify the legal and fiscal restraints that currently impede change. The federal disincentives to deinstitutionalization and the complex funding patterns of decentralized services are documented in Chapter 5. Changes in this area can be fostered by strong advocacy groups that can influence decision makers at the state and national levels.

Another important approach to facilitating change is to develop practical staff retraining and relocation mechanisms. Many people have devoted their professional lives to working in institutions. If they are shifted to decentralized systems, which may be entirely foreign to their mode of operation, it is essential that they be provided with *effective* training and relocation. This provides an excellent opportunity for consumer and legal organizations to join forces with unions in designing and implementing training programs.

It is important to identify and/or to develop and publicize model prototypes of a truly desirable spectrum of community-based residential services. Models are needed not only of programs but also of effective and efficient management and administrative systems. These models should be particularly sensitive to issues of authority, accountability, and funding.

Adoption of community-based residential services would also be encouraged by sound research evidence validating their desirability. Research to date is scanty and often equivocal. Important research questions need to be answered to provide greater empirical support for proposed changes. For example, the following research questions illustrate the types of studies desperately needed:

What is the effect of different types of residential settings on different types of retarded persons at different stages of their lives? What are the long-range consequences?

What is the impact on family members of different patterns of residential services for the retarded member of the family?

What are the cost-benefit implications of different types of residential settings?

What are the potential applications of specially designed environments incorporating principles of bioengineering for profoundly retarded and multiply handicapped persons?

What are the potential implications of specialized communications devices (e.g., Yerkish and Blissymbols) with nonverbal, severly handicapped persons?

To what degree is biofeedback technology applicable to severely handicapped retarded individuals?

What is the effect of group size and composition on persons with different types and degrees of handicaps?

The success of community-based services is predicated, in part at least, on continued expansion and refinement of technology. It is alarming that some professionals argue that since current technology is unsuccessful in training certain individuals, these people are untrainable. Rather that returning to self-fulfilling concepts of "untrainable" people, it is far preferable to attribute lack of success to a technology still in its infancy. Frustrations in training programs should be a catalyst to improving current technology rather than a rationalization for abandoning training efforts.

Thus, systems based on self-fulfilling and self-limiting prophecies that are predicated on our current technological limitations should be rejected. Otherwise there is a real danger of returning to the time when erudite professionals evaluated retarded persons and made omnipotent decisions as to which person was or was not a candidate for training. Under this regressive model, people judged not to be candidates for training would likely be assigned—perhaps for the rest of their lives—to what the Partlow "experts" refer to as an "enriched living" experience (*Wyatt* v. *Aderholt*, Motion for Modification, 1978). This enriched living experience is not too different from what institutions have allegedly tried to provide for the past 60 years. It is highly questionable that today's professionals know enough about human beings to decide who can and who cannot respond to a rapidly expanding technology.

Finally, it is important to recognize that the success of community-based residential services is predicated on effective approaches to modifying public behavior. Attitudes may be an ephemeral concept, and, as such, they may be quite difficult to modify. Behavior, on the other hand, can be operationally defined, and technology is now available for its modification. Many of the problems described by Knight (Chapter 9) were the result of destructive behavior by people in communities. It would be extremely helpful to apply behavior modification to change the social matrix within which mentally retarded citizens will be living.

SUMMARY

Many people cherish the past, resent the present, and fear the future. As documented in this chapter, the future is often a source of confusion and anxiety, resulting in anger, frustration, supersimplification, denial, withdrawal, and rationalization. But human beings are unique in that they can dream, develop ideologies, and imagine how things should be rather than how they are. These fantasies and hopes also lie in the future. Human beings are unique in that they have the power to change what is, to shape the future, and to design their own destinies so that their dreams can become realities.

REFERENCES

Allport, G. W. 1937. Personality, A Psychological Interpretation. Holt, Rinehart & Winston, Inc., New York.

National Association for Retarded Citizens. 1977. Survey Analysis, AAL Project. Improving Residential Services (unpublished). Arlington, Tex.

Nihira, L., and Nihira, K. 1975. Jeopardy in community placement. Am. J. Ment. Defic. 79:538–544.

Perls, F. 1973. The Gestalt Approach and Eye Witness to Therapy. Science and Behavior Books, Inc., Palo Alto, Cal.

Roos, P. 1969. Current Issues in Residential Care. National Association for Retarded Citizens. Arlington, Tex.

Roos, P. 1970. Evolutionary changes of the residential facility. In: A. Baumeister and E. Butterfield (eds.), Residential Facilities for the Mentally Retarded, pp. 29–58. Aldine Publishing Company, Chicago.

Roos, P. 1972. Mentally retarded citizens: Challenge for the 1970s. Syracuse Law Rev. 23:1059–1074.

Roos, P. 1979. The law and mentally retarded people: An uncertain future. Stanford Law Rev. 31(4):613–624.

Roos, P., and McCann, B. 1977. Major trends in mental retardation. Intl. J. Ment. Health 6:3–20.

Toffler, A. 1970. Future Shock. Random House, Inc., New York.

3

ASSESSING PROGRAMMATIC ASPECTS OF THE PROBLEM

Charles J. Seevers

Vanier often speaks of the "double wound" suffered by the retarded person. There is the organic wound from a given combination of genes or from an accident of birth. But the second wound, that of rejection, is much greater (Vanier, 1972). Rejection takes many forms.

One night the author received an emergency phone call about a 19-year-old mentally retarded woman who was home alone because her mother, dying of cancer, had been taken to the hospital. The young lady was assured that some emergency provision could be made. The next night the mother died. This resulted in a 19-year-old retarded woman, with low verbal abilities, confused, and frightened by incomprehensible events, at home alone. She needed immediate admission into a residential service system. The official state system allowed only one alternative—a state hospital. She was physically well and did not need a hospital. Just a place to live.

If she had been a resident in the Washington D.C. area, she might have been sent to Forest Haven in Laurel, Maryland. There, as reported by Anderson (1978) in his *Washington Merry-Go-Round*, she might have been placed in Dogwood Cottage.

> Dogwood was a veritable snakepit. I once witnessed a nurse open a cottage door only to find 80 half-clad screaming women come running to the door; the nurse quickly shut it. . . . Other patients are chemically restrained, that is, they are given large doses of the dreaded drug, Thorazine. . . . This leaves them sleepy, lifeless, still (Anderson, 1978).

The needs of such dependent people thrust suddenly into an incomprehensibly isolated life space, and alternatives like Forest Haven that decision makers have designed, make an examination essential of the entire decision process and underscore the need for responsible assessments that will more accurately specify true needs of individuals who are depending upon others to make decisions in their best developmental interests.

But therein lies a problem. Bennis et al. (1976) point out an Achilles heel in the decision-making process that yields outcomes like Forest Haven. Typically, decision makers when confronted with a problem review available facts, decide to accept them at the moment, proceed with the decision process, and emerge with solutions that are more often than not based upon *their* interpretation of one's needs. In effect, they and the quality of their decisions are accountable only to themselves, since their claim to represent an individual in the decision space rests upon their interpretation of that person's needs as they relate to the system in general and not necessarily to the person in question.

THE NEED FOR CAREFUL ASSESSMENT

In a very real sense, therefore, how decisions are made about clients becomes more important than predicting and measuring program outcomes. Pappas et al. (1976) raised some key questions: Is planning based on the client's needs? Are individual plans being written? Are they being reviewed? Who has input into the planning and review process? These and other questions are integral components of systematic and individual assessment leading to more precise and objective decisions.

In searching for a community system that will best meet the needs of the 19-year-old woman described above, if Forest Haven is not the answer, what criteria can be used by decision makers to find the best answer? Initially, they might follow the four criteria for a community system listed by Wolfensberger (1972):

1. Programs for retarded individuals should be *dispersed* throughout the larger community as much as possible.
2. Services for retarded individuals should be *specialized* to meet unique configurations of individual needs.
3. Services for retarded citizens should be *integrated* into comparable services for the nonretarded population to the greatest extent possible.
4. The system must provide *continuity* in both inter-agency and intra-agency functions.

Assessing a given community's adherence to these four criteria is not sufficient for making a formal decision. There is also a need to explore the values that guide the decision making of the service providers in the system.

Pappas et al. (1976) have identified a set of five values central to true deinstitutionalization that are to be used as a guide for decision making:

1. That each person's unique traits and behaviors are to be celebrated and built upon rather than adjusted or changed
2. That each person should be an active participant in life rather than the subject of another's control
3. That each person should have access to the settings which allow for continual growth
4. That each person can learn to make his environment responsive to his personal needs and inclinations, through consultation and feedback
5. That each person can make some kind of contribution to his life environment

If the goal was to deinstitutionalize the Forest Haven residents, it becomes apparent that "deinstitutionalization" takes on a more complex meaning. It does not simply imply that a person is physically transferred from a state hospital to a community facility.

> Instead, deinstitutionalization deals with the process of opening up less routinized and more varied behaviors for both individuals and for settings, no matter *what* the facility or *where* it is. According to this view, former hospital residents moved to smaller but still highly restricted community settings are not deinstitutionalized. In such cases, there has been decentralization of facilities, but not deinstitutionalization of persons. Broadly, deinstitutionalization is a reorganization of services in order to open a larger set of alternatives for handicapped people in the community. But what must underlie and link to this is another aspect of the deinstitutionalization process, and that concerns the person (Pappas et al., 1976).

· Whether decisions are being made with regard to the Forest Haven residents or the person whose mother had just died, the first step is responsible and thorough assessment of the individual. Dybwad (1974) has frequently championed the individuality of the handicapped person. NARC publications (National Association for Retarded Citizens, 1973) have repeatedly asserted that "program objectives should be tailored to meet the needs of each individual and will vary for different degrees of impairment." O'Connor (1976) has asserted: "Each developmentally disabled person residing in a community residential facility or in any other type of community placement, should have a comprehensive developmental plan made." This plan should be based on a "careful evaluation of the abilities as well as the disabilities of the individual, and include prescriptive steps toward the attainment of increasingly independent levels of functioning." Norley (1972) contends that the system classically assumes that the retarded person is nonchanging. Retarded individuals do change. That is probably why there is no "ideal" service system in which the fit between the needs of the clients and of the system is perfect. But the service is worth little unless it is a part of a delivery structure that makes it available to *all* who need it *when* they need it and in a *form* that is useful (Paul, Weigerink, and Neufeld, 1974).

ASSESSMENT UNDER THE DEVELOPMENTAL MODEL

It has become obvious to decision makers that individual assessment is the critical link to their task in order to establish baselines and to later measure any change as a result of the actions taken to implement their decisions.

Seevers (1975c) has designed a prototype for evaluating the effects of group home living through individual assessments of the members. The developmental model paradigm (Figure 1) graphically depicts an evaluation taxonomy for the five developmental growth areas based upon the assumption that retarded persons have more than physical needs, to the extent that a person can respond to training in one or more of these five developmental growth areas from infancy to old age. The person can grow more self-reliant within society.

Measurement instruments for identifying the level of growth achieved in each of the five developmental growth areas are used as part of the diagnostic and evaluation sequence. Upon entry into the residential unit, each resident receives an assessment that identifies baseline development in each of the five growth areas. The staff of Aux Chandelles (located in Bristol, Indiana), which operates residential facilities, has utilized all of the instruments listed in the paradigm and has found the Gunzburg (1976) *Progress Assessment Charts* (PAC) from England to be the most universally objective and practical assessment instrument for the local community. One of the more helpful features of the PAC is the psychogram (Figure 2), which graphically demonstrates changes and rate of progress in acquisition of skills leading toward increased social competency. A personal assessment psychogram facilitates establishing baseline data for developing affective growth objectives for the individualized program plan (IPP). Part 2 of the *adaptive behavior scale* (Nihira et al., 1974) is also used for ascertaining affective growth goals.

Following the assessment of the individual clients, an overall program assessment can begin. Interdisciplinary team reviews of client program plans ensure goal-oriented programming that is kept in tune with client needs, staffing patterns, and facilities to meet program requirements. Specific approaches and objectives are always modified or replaced as a result of these program measurements. Careful assessment and reassessment is necessary to ensure that approaches and objectives are meeting needs and moving toward previously established goals.

Client needs may or may not be fulfilled without a realistic measure of progress. Residential programs may mistakenly appear appropriate without careful and thorough assessment at regular intervals. A personal experience of the author illustrates this point.

Five years ago, a typical mid-America county, half rural and half urban, found itself initiating community-based residential service. Existing programs from Nebraska to Connecticut and from Great Britain to Scandinavia were carefully evaluated. Decisions were made that, it was hoped, would meet the needs of an orphaned woman as well as institutionalized former residents of the county. One particular experience in the process underscores the need for ongoing program assessment in order to truly meet future client needs.

The evolution of staffing patterns in some of the initiated residential facilities resulted in a transition from a live-in houseparent model to a shift basis of employment. On the surface, the shift system appeared to be working well. Staff members seemed to cope better with regular 8-hour shifts that allowed them to return to their homes at the end of each shift, apparently avoiding the burnout syndrome.

A closer assessment, however, indicated that client needs were not being met adequately. Clients were forced to relate to numerous staff; IPP objectives development was poor; communication discrepancies and gaps were evidenced between shifts, resulting in unmet client needs; and emphasis seemed to be centered around staff needs rather than client needs. The staff appeared to be more attached to their particular shifts than to a concern for the overall appearance and functioning of the homes and clients.

Without careful assessment of client growth, this situation would likely have continued, or have been modified inappropriately. Thought was given to modifying and more closely monitoring the shift system, but at best it appeared that the system would fall short of meeting the ideology of a normative environment. It was reasoned that normal families do not have three sets of parents, each walking in every 8 hours for their shifts. Thus, the decision was made to go back to the live-in model, where the overall responsibility of the home was assigned to one live-in houseparent. More pride was soon evidenced as the staff developed a close relationship to their own home and "family" and more

---

A DEVELOPMENTAL MODEL
PARADIGM FOR EVALUATION AND
DECISION MAKING

IDEOLOGICAL RATIONALE

   It would seem essential that when decision-makers are confronted with human beings whose human needs require human solutions, an ideological base might be determined which would best facilitate identification of the total problem and development of the best solution.

   For example, when a person's natural home terminates, for whatever reason—poverty, handicap—outside shelter has been provided in a state institution or county home. Traditionally, these institutions have, to one degree or another, operated under a Custodial Model whereas the vast majority of residents need a Developmental Model. Potential differences between the two models might be described as follows:

Custodial Model	*Developmental Model*
Person is "IT"	Person is "He" or "She"
Focus on what's wrong	Focus on what's possible
Treatment of disabilities	Development of abilities
Passive behavior (chemotherapy)	Active behavior (positive)
Physiological	Psychological
Separate from community	Integrate in community
Emphasis on "illness"	Emphasis on growth
Dehumanize	Humanize

   The Custodial Model is oriented around *treatment* of the handicapped as opposed to the Developmental Model which is oriented around the respective capacities for *growth.*

   The Developmental Model takes an optimistic view of the modification of behavior. It is not concentrated on differences. It operates under the assumption that the developmentally disabled person is capable of growth.

DEVELOPMENTAL MODEL PARADIGM

   If a retarded person has more than physical needs, what are they and how can they be identified? There are 5 basic developmental growth areas.

MOTOR
   Balance and posture
   Perceptual motor
   Locomotion
   Body image (psychosexual)
   Psychophysical
   Manipulative skills
SOCIAL
   Self-help
   Self-care
   Social behavior toward others (Interpersonal)
   Safety
COMMUNICATION
   Non-verbal
   Verbal
AFFECTIVE
   Emotions
   Feelings
COGNITIVE
   Intellectual and number skills
   Basic knowledge
   Practical skills
   Economic activity

   To the extent that a person can respond to training in one or more of these areas from infancy to old age, to that extent he can grow—learn—and develop into a more capable person, and a happier, less dependent member of society .

   Measurement instruments utilized for purposes of identifying the level of growth achieved in each of the 5 developmental growth areas are utilized as part of a diagnostic and evaluation sequence.

Figure 1.   A developmental model paradigm for evaluation and decision making. (Source: Seevers, C. J. 1975c. Program assessment chart. In: A Schroeder (ed.), Agency Self-Evaluation in the Community, pp. 31–36. Proceedings from the Workshop, Developmental Training Center, Indiana University, Bloomington. Reprinted by permission.)

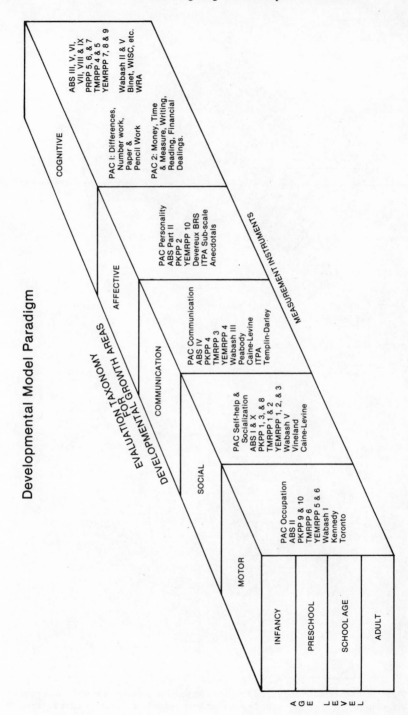

Developmental Model Paradigm

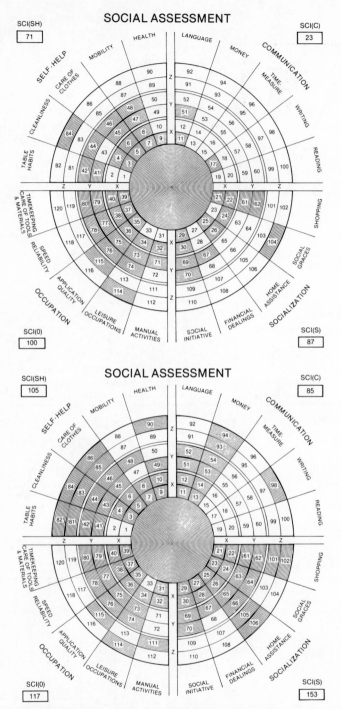

Figure 2.   Sparkhill Project. The Progress of Elizabeth shown in the social and personal diagrams of PAC 2. Upper half, first assessments; lower half, latest assessments. (Source:

PERSONAL ASSESSMENT

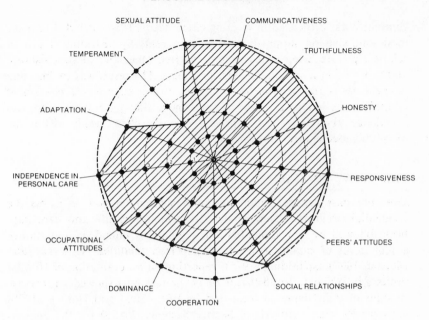

PERSONAL ASSESSMENT

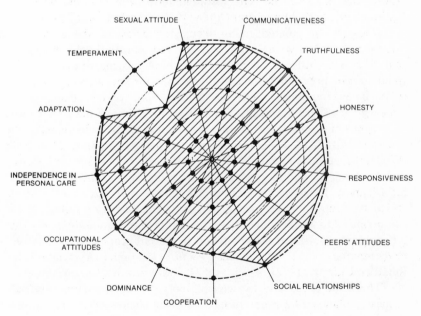

Gunzburg, H. C. 1975. Institutionalized people in the community. REAP 1:36-50.
Reprinted by permission.)

continuity was evidenced in meeting client needs. It was decided to place more emphasis on supporting the houseparents by providing improved salaries, private living spaces, regulated free time, and more assistance and expertise in handling behavior problems. The result was the meeting of client needs and happier houseparents. In this experience, assessment of individuals led to a program assessment that gave more empirical knowledge about the best approach to meet client needs within the program's ideological value system.

THE "HOW" TO ASSESS

Over the past decade, much has been written on how to assess the residential program. "New models for community life and care have been followed by new standards and regulations intended to guarantee a high level of quality control in dispersed facilities" (Pilovsky and Matson, 1977). Spaulding (1975), reporting on an evaluation of 10 pilot projects in Indiana, found that 91% of the residents showed an increase in skills of daily living as measured by PAC. Heal and Daniels (1978) used the Program Analysis of Service Systems (PASS) for the analysis of residential alternatives in Wisconsin. Gini (1976) reviewed some failures that materialized. Other studies have been reported by Elwyn Institute (1972), Wehbring and Ogren (1976), and Bergman (1974).

Roos (1970) pointed to an increasing array of sheltered living arrangements that were being evolved, but appropriately mentioned that there was little or no research evidence bearing directly on this trend toward provision of living alternatives for the mentally retarded in the open community. The few studies that are now beginning to appear in the literature need to be followed with many more that focus on program assessment based upon assessment of the individuals in the program. *PASS, A Program Anaysis of Service Systems Handbook* (Wolfensberger and Glenn, 1975) can be used to measure an approximation to normalized life-styles. The Accreditation Council for Services for Mentally Retarded and Other Developmentally Disabled Persons (1978) has published a broad and comprehensive set of standards for community and residential services. Another basic evaluative checklist for program assessment may be found in the publication *Developmental Programming in the Residential Facility* (National Association for Retarded Citizens, 1972), which lists 246 yes/no evaluation questions.

These standards and assessment tools can be used quantitatively to measure how well a program meets a given client's needs. It is essential that they be used regularly because it is possible to create a truly normative environment, complying with all legal requirements, that is inadequate if it does not truly meet the client's needs. Institutions, group homes, and so on, are neither good nor bad just because they exist.

Places like Forest Haven began because somebody was trying to solve a problem. The residential alternative of a century ago, or the system designed a decade ago, may no longer be adequate. Decision makers must forego the temptation to develop facilities and systems and then simply make present and future clients fit into them. Rather, they should identify client needs and see how facilities or systems can be modified, restructured, or replaced to meet those needs. A residential system can be evaluated in terms of how well it adheres to philosophical principles, standards, legal guidelines, and societal needs but the true measure is: *What are the real client needs and are they being met?*

This advocation may appear to be obvious and too "trivial" to expound upon. However, as an example, the author was involved in developing an apartment fourplex designed to meet the needs of clients who had benefited from group home training, and needed a less restrictive alternative that would allow them to "polish up" their skills before moving on to more independent living situations in the community. The system was set, was in compliance with all standards and legal guidelines, and initially *did* assist individuals with their needs. However, the changing needs of incoming clients were such that they could not benefit from this semi-independent living construct. It would have been easy to continue with what was and still is a quality structured program for certain needs. In identifying current individual needs, however, the programmatic structure of the fourplex was modified and is now used to meet a different set of needs as required by incoming clients.

ASSESSMENT OF THE LEAST RESTRICTIVE ALTERNATIVE

The concept of least restrictive alternative was identified as a crucial dynamic that needed to be objectified or operationalized in some way to best serve the individuals and to make decisions regarding staff, facilities, and allocation of dollars.

In a search of the literature, it was found that "the least restrictive alternative" was frequently mentioned as a concept, but it did not seem to raise a single connotation or promote a unified course of action for service providers. In fact, Switzky and Miller (1978) believe that "implementation of the procedure as it now exists may place many service providers in a serious dilemma since the concept of the least restrictive alternative is only partially defined and thus only partially understood." They cite Chambers (1974): "If the feasibility of attaining goals is an important criteria for judging a situation's ultimate restrictiveness, then the wrong criteria are often used in ascertaining program restrictiveness" (p. 51). The author and his colleagues felt that operationalizing the least restrictive alternative required specifying behavioral goals and then matching the environments that would optimize the likelihood of achieving mutually agreed upon terminal skills. Pappas et al. (1976) have pointed out that what is too restrictive for one person may be the least restrictive for another.

What are the variables to be considered? It is necessary to begin by assessing the client needs and then the residential system designed to meet those needs. Such an assessment would include:

1. An *assessment of each client's skills*, including a determination of levels of restrictiveness
2. An identification of the *least restrictive alternative* for the client based on his needs and "level of restrictiveness"
3. Identification of the client's *current residential alternative* and its level of restrictiveness
4. A *comparison* between the alternative that is *needed* (see 2 above) with the one in which the client resides (3 above)

The ideal then, is a quantitative measure of the discrepancy between 2 (the client's *needed* level of restrictiveness) and 3 (the client's *current* level of restrictiveness). A hypothetical result could be as follows:

> Client: John Smith
> Level of restrictiveness needed   35%
> Level of restrictiveness of his current environment   75%
> Difference   40%
> The current environment is 40% too restrictive.

This computation would be completed for all clients in the residential system, and an overall score could be computed. This would indicate what overall and specific changes need to be made. Once the discrepancies are identified, it is possible to proceed with:

5. Normalization and other principles
6. Standards compliance
7. Staffing needs
8. Facility needs
9. Funding needs

The Trace matrix, designed by Michael Trace, Director of Residential Services, Aux Chandelles (Figure 3), can objectify residential placement decisions within the context of the least restrictive alternative. It uses selected scales of currently existing developmental assessment tools. Utilization of the matrix can provide:

1. A quantitative determination of the level of restrictiveness of an individual's *current residential alternative* (CRA)
2. A quantitative determination of the level of restrictiveness of what would be the individual's *least restrictive alternative* (LRA)

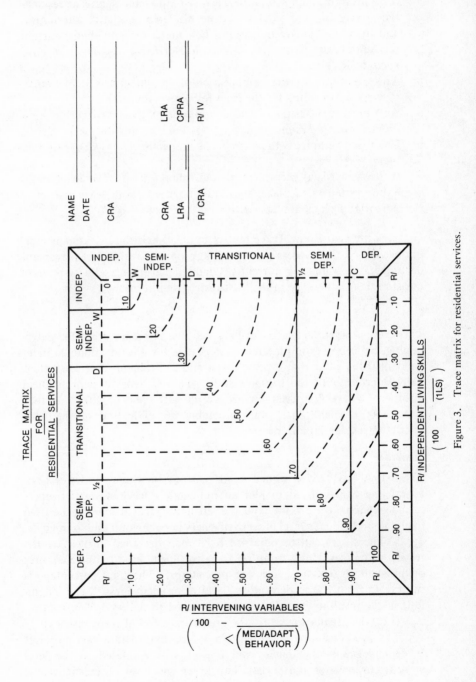

Figure 3.   Trace matrix for residential services.

33

3. A quantitative comparison between the individual's current residential alternative and what would be his least restrictive alternative, and thus an objective measure of how much an individual's current residential alternative is *either too restrictive or not restrictive enough* (R/DIFF)
4. An overall quantitative computation of a residential *system's effectiveness* in providing for the least restrictive alternative
5. An objective measure of the *continuum of placement needs of a given residential population* (e.g., waiting lists, institutions)
6. The type of emphasis to be stressed on a person's *individual program plan*
7. An overall visual picture of an individual's level of independence, appropriateness of placement, training needs, and least restrictive potential placement alternative

It is the goal of the Trace matrix to blend existing assessment tools in objectifying the process of making appropriate residential placement decisions and evaluating current residential placements and systems to measure their adherence to the least restrictive alternative.

Concept

The Trace residential matrix utilizes two measurement areas for determining the appropriate placement alternative for an individual: 1) independent living skills that a person has, and 2) problems that can potentially interfere with the person's skills, that is, behavioral or medical disorders. These two variables are graphically conceptualized as they interact with each other, thus providing an indication of the least restrictive residential alternative.

Structure

The matrix has been designed to form a box in which the lower horizontal line can be used to plot an individual's level of restrictiveness in independent living skills, and the left-hand vertical line can be used to plot an individual's level of restrictiveness in behavioral and/or medical needs. The scores can be obtained from tools designed to measure the respective indices (PAC, Adaptive Behavior Scale, etc.), with raw scores modified to be scored in terms of percentages. The total percentage is subtracted from 100 to determine "level of restrictiveness." The magnitude of the resultant score is positively related to the level of restrictiveness (i.e., the greater the score, the greater the level of restrictiveness).

The two remaining sides of the box are divided into varying levels of dependence-independence, and are negatively related to the level of restrictiveness of the scales. The lower the level of restrictiveness of each scale, the greater the level of independence equated on the opposite line.

We then have a box that would appear similar to that shown in Figure 4. The box is further divided into sections to represent the identified levels of independence.

These levels—dependent, semi-dependent, marginal, semi-independent, and independent—are then associated with the amount of client supervision to be structured into each level (e.g., continuous supervision for those in a dependent setting; continuous to once per half-day for those in a semi-dependent setting; half-day to once per day for those in a marginal setting; once a day to once a week for those in a semi-independent setting; and once a week or less for those in an independent setting). These levels are defined by the scores obtained on the scales of the matrix and indicate how a respective residential alternative should be structured.

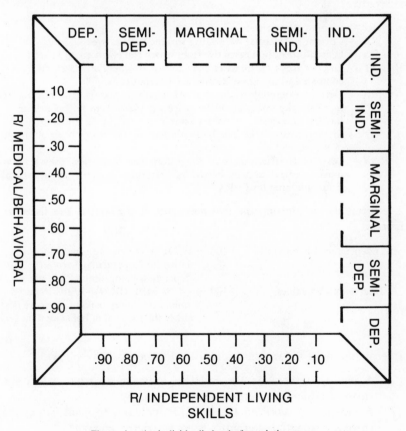

Figure 4.   An individual's level of restrictiveness.

In such a matrix, the upper right-hand corner represents total independence (a score of 0), and the lower left-hand corner total dependence (a score of 100). The dotted lines within the matrix represent, in percentages, the distance away from 0 (and thus, the distance away from total independence).

The level of restrictiveness of an individual for independent living skills can be plotted on the lower horizontal line, and the level of restrictiveness for interfering variables (called medical and behavioral adaptivity) on the left-hand vertical line. The point at which these two measures would intersect within the box can then be plotted, indicating an individual's overall level of restrictiveness. This can be expressed quantitatively by relating it to the closest dotted line, which indicates the distance away from total independence.

Interpretation The abbreviations included for interpreting the matrix enable scoring of the critical variables relating to least restrictive alternative:

R/ = Level of Restrictiveness
CRA = Current Residential Alternative in which client lives
LRA = Least Restrictive Alternative from which the client could benefit
R/DIFF = Level of Restrictiveness of the Current Residential Alternative when compared to the Least Restrictive Alternative
CPRA = Current Potential Residential Alternative, that is, the alternative in which the client could be placed if there were no behavioral or medical interfering variables (this score would be equal to R/ of the Independent Living Skills plotted on the lower horizontal line of the matrix)
R/IV = Level of Restrictiveness of the Interfering Variables, that is, how much medical and/or behavioral variables prohibit an individual from obtaining his CPRA

The formulas for plotting the two measures of the matrix are listed as follows:

R/Independent Living Skills   100 − (% ILS) = One hundred minus the individual's percentage score for independent living skills (PAC, etc.)

R/Intervening Variables   100 − (< % MED/BEH) = One hundred minus the lesser percentage score of either the medical or behavioral measures

Interpretations of the various scores can then be made as follows:

1. A plus (+) score on the R/DIFF indicates to what extent the current residential alternative is too restrictive.
2. A minus (−) score on the R/DIFF indicates to what extent the current residential alternative is not restrictive enough.

3. A zero (0) score on the R/DIFF indicates there are no extraneous variables interfering with an individual's current potential for residential placement.

4. A plus (+) score on the R/IV indicates to what extent interfering variables are inhibiting an individual's current potential for residential placement.

5. A plus (+) score on the R/IV indicates that the individual's program plan should place an emphasis on counseling, behavior modification, medical intervention, and other techniques used to eliminate maladaptive behavior and medical difficulties. A plus (+) score on the R/IV also limits an individual's potential to decrease his R/Independent Living Skills.

6. A zero (0) score on the R/IV indicates that an individual's program plan should place an emphasis on training in independent living skills—and also indicates maximum potential to decrease his R/Independent Living Skills.

7. In addition to the plus or minus score on the R/DIFF, one can determine visually on the matrix the appropriateness of the CRA (distance between the CRA and the LRA, and the location on the independence continuum of both the CRA and the LRA).

8. In addition to the score on the R/IV, the emphasis needed on the IPP can be determined visually from the matrix. (The scores listed on the matrix that indicate the percentage for the LRA form a visual line dividing the matrix. Any LRA below this line indicates an IPP need for counseling, etc., while any LRA on or above this line indicates an IPP need for training in independent living skills.)

9. The overall level of independence of the client can also be determined visually on the matrix, and repeated administration of the matrix can indicate general direction of progress.

10. Quantitatively, and visually, the overall R/DIFF provided by a given residential system can be determined.

11. Quantitatively, and visually, the residential placement needs of a given residential population can be determined (institutions, waiting lists, etc.).

Steps   It should be noted that the utility of the matrix is only as effective as the tools used to measure the two variables—independent living skills and behavioral/medical needs. The matrix is structured so that agencies can use their own assessment tools in measuring independent living skills and adaptive behavior. If such tools exist, agencies need only adjust them so that percentage scores can be computed based on the percentage of skills that have been acquired. The PAC has been found effective in measuring independent living skills, as exemplified below, and Part II of the Adaptive Behavior Scale, along with the Personal Assessment part of the PAC, has been effective in measuring the behavioral continuum. At this point, a scale for medical needs has not been identified, and this dimension is thus limited to subjective evaluation (are there medical/physical needs that restrict the individual's independence, such as uncontrolled seizures?).

The steps below summarize the required procedures in using the matrix and are developed around the use of the PAC and Adaptive Behavior Scale as assessment tools.

1. *Plot on the lower horizontal line the level of restrictiveness (R/) for independent living skills.* This will be 100 minus the percentage score for independent living skills (see Figure 4). In using the PAC, an Independent Living Skills Profile has been devised (Figure 5) that highlights those skills primarily attributable to independent living. A card is made that is placed over the PAC psychogram, allowing the evaluator to see the scoring for only the designated independent living skills. The evaluator simply adds the number of full and partial competencies and multiplies this by 1.85, resulting in a percentage score (which will be 100 if all skills were acquired). This score is subtracted from 100, and the resulting score is plotted on the matrix.

2. *Plot on the left-hand vertical line the level of restrictiveness (R/) for the intervening variables (behavioral/medical).* This will normally be 100 minus the smaller percentage score of either the behavioral or medical variable (i.e., the one that is the most restrictive). For adaptive behavior, this can be computed on the PAC by taking 1.54 times the total of the points plotted on the personal assessment. This score is then subtracted from 100. Part II of the Adaptive Behavior Scale may also be used by simply plotting the actual percentage of the highest score (excluding medical) as summarized on the Profile Summary or Data Summary Sheet. On this measure, the evaluator will want to pay attention to the relative importance of the interfering variables, and adjust accordingly.

Until an effective tool is realized for medical interference, the evaluator may make a listing of the medical problems and determine which are restrictive (i.e., cannot be overcome). It is then possible to determine how much assistance or dependence the client requires (how long can the person be left alone?) and to find this on the dependence-independence scale directly across from the interfering variable scale. This index can be related to the percentage score directly across from it on the interfering variable scale, and the medical or behavioral score that is the larger is then actually plotted.

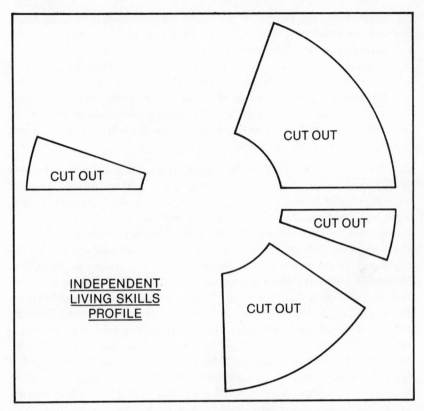

Figure 5.   Independent living skills profile.

3. *Plot within the matrix the appropriate Least Restrictive Alternative (LRA) for the individual.* This is determined by locating the point within the matrix at which R/Independent Living Skills and R/Interfering Variables would intersect if extended perpendicularly to their respective scales. This point can be translated quantitatively by noting its relative position to the scaled dotted lines within the matrix.

4. *Plot the Current Residential Alternative (CRA) in which the individual lives.* This can be done by considering the type of facility and the level of supervision it provides (e.g., if it is a nursing home that provides continuous supervision, this would be plotted at approximately .90). If supervision ranges from continuous to once each half-day, the evaluator would plot the facility somewhere in the semi-dependent range. When in doubt about the specific plotting within a range (e.g., semi-independent), select the point *within* the range that is closest to the established least restrictive alternative

(thus giving the benefit of the doubt that the level of restrictiveness can be provided). This CRA plotting can also be quantified and recorded on the right-hand portion of the form where indicated.

5. *Complete computations.* This is done on the right-hand portion of the form. LRA is subtracted from CRA to get R/DIFF. CPRA can be recorded (same score as R/Independent Living Skills) and subtracted from LRA to get R/IV. These scores can then be compared, and other analyses completed as discussed in the narrative above under *Interpretations.*

Examples The matrices described below and illustrated in Figures 6-10 provide examples of the computations as completed on an individual who actually progressed through a series of residential placements that were both too restrictive and not restrictive enough.

Matrix 1 At the time that the author became involved with C.D., she was a resident of a local nursing home. This was a significantly dependent environment and is plotted within the matrix at .90 (CRA) (Figure 6). However, administration of a PAC on C.D. found her independent living skills percentage to be .72, which resulted in a level of restrictiveness of .28 (plotted on the lower horizontal line of the matrix). In addition, C.D. had no interfering medical problems (she was prone to seizures, but these were controlled by medication that she could take herself) and received an adaptive behavior score of .79, which resulted in a level of restrictiveness of .21 (plotted on the left-hand vertical line of the matrix). The resultant least restrictive alternative (LRA) was then located at .24 within the matrix by plotting the intersection of the above restrictiveness scores. Thus, at this time, C.D.'s residential alternative was .90, and her least restrictive alternative was .24, resulting in a +.66 score for restrictiveness of the current residential alternative (R/DIFF), which was far too restrictive. Plans were thus made to move C.D. into a group home that more closely approximated her least restrictive alternative.

Matrix 2 C.D. was ultimately placed in a group home in January 1975, and the matrix in Figure 7 was completed the following October. At this point, her CRA was .30, and her LRA was computed to be .22, resulting in an R/DIFF of +.08, which was not significant. Given the R/ of .13 for her independent living skills, her current *potential* least restrictive alternative (CPRA) was .13. In comparing this with her *actual* needed least restrictive alternative, she received an R/IV of −.09, indicating that the interfering variables (problems in adaptive behavior) somewhat limited her progress.

Because her actual skills were so high, it was decided to move C.D. into a less restrictive setting (independent apartment) in hopes that the lower level of restrictiveness might eliminate the problems connected with the interfering variables.

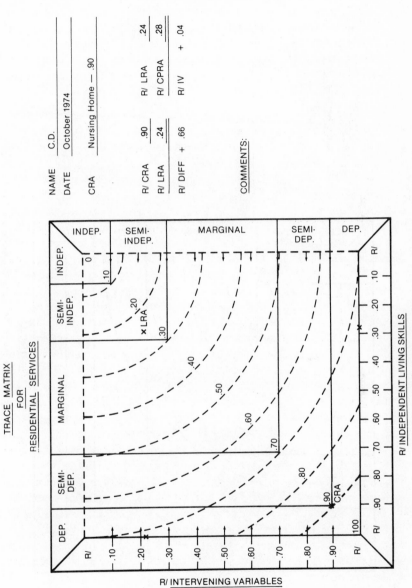

Figure 6.   C.D.'s original Trace matrix for residential services.

TRACE MATRIX
FOR
RESIDENTIAL SERVICES

NAME   C.D.
DATE   October 1974

CRA   Nursing Home — .90

R/ CRA   .90   R/ LRA   .24
R/ LRA   .24   R/ CPRA   .28
R/ DIFF + .66   R/ IV   +   .04

COMMENTS:

INDEP.   SEMI-INDEP.   MARGINAL   SEMI-DEP.   DEP.

R/ INDEPENDENT LIVING SKILLS

R/ INTERVENING VARIABLES

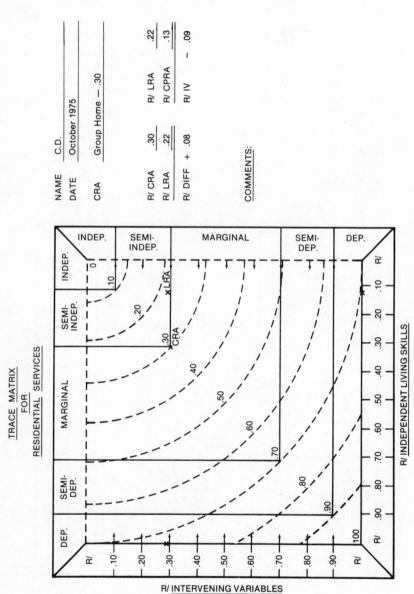

Figure 7. C.D.'s Trace matrix for residential services in October 1975.

42

Matrix 3 A third matrix (Figure 8) was completed on C.D.'s placement in December 1975, and it was discovered that the move to the apartment was inappropriate. She continued to have behavior problems, as reflected on her R/Interfering Variable of .28, and her LRA was plotted at .22. Given her CRA of .10, the resultant R/DIFF of −.12 indicated that the environment was not restrictive enough. This continued, and C.D. was eventually moved back into the group home.

Matrix 4 In May 1978, following further training and counseling, the matrix (Figure 9) indicated that C.D. might finally be ready to move out of the group home. Her R/Independent Living Skills was lowered to .07 and her R/Interfering Variables was reduced to .18. The resultant LRA was .12, resulting in an R/DIFF of +.18. Thus, C.D. moved out into an apartment.

Matrix 5 The matrix shown in Figure 10, which was completed in November 1978, indicates that C.D.'s apartment placement was successful. Her CRA is .10 and her LRA was computed at .08. In addition, her R/IV was reduced to 0. C.D. continues in this placement.

As may be seen, the Trace matrix is an assessment tool that objectifies and operationalizes the crucial least restrictive alternative concept.

CONCLUSION

A mother died suddenly. A 19-year-old woman found herself incomprehensibly alone in the midst of her community.

A door opened and 80 half-clad, screaming women came running to the door. The door was quickly shut.

Unless a viable community-based range of residential home-like settings are provided for the retarded and other developmentally disabled persons, the poor and helpless will continue to be committed to state warehouses, penitentiaries, and reform schools and placed under the surveillance of courts and probation officers. People will also continue to be added to the welfare rolls, an indecent dependency with its resulting degradation of the human spirit. Impairment and poverty, coupled with idleness and loneliness, invariably lead to trouble and to some kind of imprisonment.

In light of the gifts and resources available today, basic human concern for impaired persons places upon society the responsibility to create a decent alternative for the disabled victims who continue to fill our archaic and inhumane institutions. Community-based homes with supportive client services will not only eliminate most of the degradations suffered by the less fortunate victims of public indifference, but will also enable them to enter the mainstream of life with an increasing

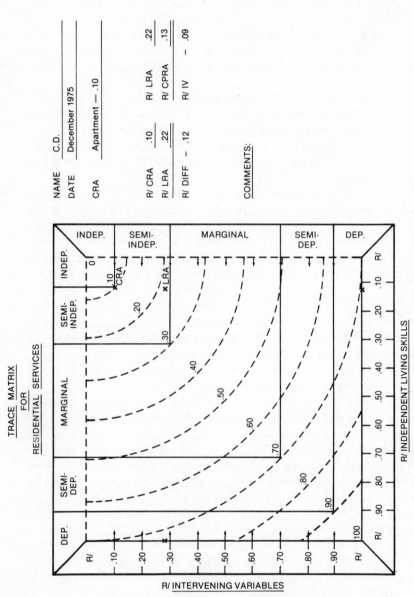

Figure 8. C.D.'s Trace matrix for residential services in December 1975.

44

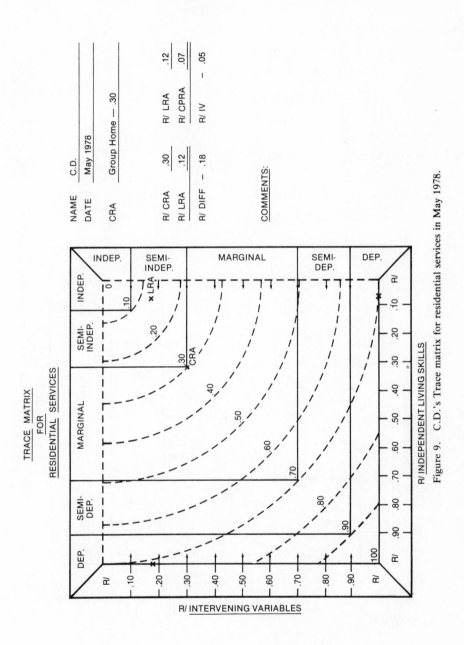

Figure 9. C.D.'s Trace matrix for residential services in May 1978.

45

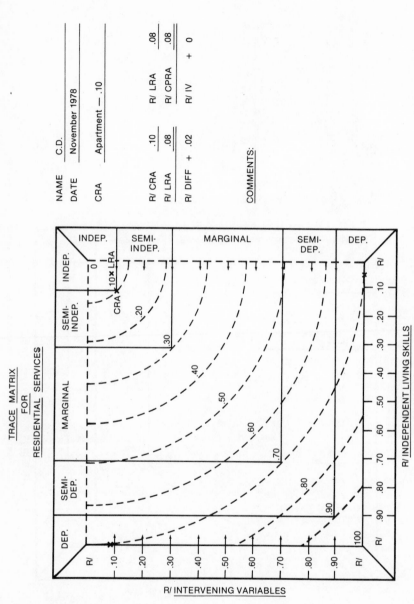

Figure 10. C.D.'s Trace matrix for residential services in November 1978.

46

independence and the dignity inherent in being a contributing member of society. It is, after all, no more than the basic American promise so well expressed by Thomas Wolfe: "To every man his chance, to every man, regardless of his birth, his shining golden opportunity—to every man the right to live, to work, to be himself, and to become whatever thing his manhood and vision can combine to make him—this, seeker, is the promise of America."

The impaired, like other citizens, are "children of the Universe—they have a right to be here" and their birthright as Americans includes, at the very least, an assessment of their individual needs, a fitting place to live, and a right to treatment as human beings by decision makers.

REFERENCES

Accreditation Council for Services for Mentally Retarded and Other Developmentally Disabled Persons. 1978. Standards for services for developmentally disabled individuals. Joint Commission on Accreditation of Hospitals, Chicago.

Anderson, J. 1978. The fate of the retarded. Washington Merry-Go-Round. Goshen News, Goshen, Ind.

Bennis, W. G., Beene, K. D., Chin, R., and Cary, K. E. 1976. The Planning of Change. 3rd ed. Holt, Rinehart & Winston, Inc., New York.

Bergman, J. S. 1974. Community Homes for the Retarded. Lexington Books, Lexington, Mass.

Chambers, D. 1974. Right to the least restrictive alternative setting for treatment. Legal Rights of the Mentally Handicapped, vol. 2. Practicing Law Institute, New York.

Dybwad, G. 1974. New patterns of living demand new patterns of service—Is normalization a feasible principle of rehabilitation? In: Models of Service for the Multi-Handicapped Adult. Proceedings of the 1973 Conference of the International Cerebral Palsy Society, New York.

Elwyn Institute. 1972. From institution to community living. Elwyn Study, prepared by the Research Utilization Branch, Office of Research and Demonstrations, Social, and Rehabilitation Services, U.S. Department of Health, Education, and Welfare, Washington, D.C.

Gini, L. 1976. Housing and Home Services for the Disabled. Harper and Row Publishers, New York.

Gunzburg, H. C. 1966. Primary Progress Assessment Chart. NSMHC Books, London, England.

Gunzburg, H. C. 1976. PAC Manual, vols. I and II. SEFA Ltd., Stratford-on-Avon, England.

Heal, L. W., and Daniels, B. 1978. A cost-effectiveness analysis of residential alternatives for selected developmentally disabled citizens of three northern Wisconsin counties. Paper presented at the 102nd Annual Meeting of the American Association on Mental Deficiency, May, Denver.

Gunzburg, H. C. 1975. Institutionalized people in the community. REAP 1:36-50.

National Association for Retarded Citizens. 1972. A developmental model for residential services. In: Residential Programming for Mentally Retarded Persons. National Association for Retarded Citizens, Arlington, Tex.

National Association for Retarded Citizens. 1973. The right to choose: Achieving residential alternatives, p. 9. National Association for Retarded Citizens, Arlington, Tex.

Nihira, K., Foster, R., Shellhaas, M., and Leland, H. 1974. AAMD Adaptive Behavior Scale (revised). American Association on Mental Deficiency, Washington, D.C.

Norley, D. 1972. Design as a non-verbal language: Self-fulfilling prophesy for the retarded, p. 7. Paper delivered at the American Institute of Architects National Convention in Houston, Tex.

O'Connor, G. 1976. Home is a good place. AAMD Monograph No. 2. American Association on Mental Deficiency, Washington, D.C.

Pappas, V. S., Masmead, V., Miller, T., and Tracey, M. 1976. Deinstitutionalization: An ecological response, p. 5. Developmental Training Center, Indiana University, Bloomington.

Paul, J. L., Weigerink, R., and Neufeld, G. R. 1974. Advocacy—A role for developmental disabilities councils. DD/Technical Assistance System, Chapel Hill, N.C.

Pilovsky, D., and Matson, J. 1977. Community colleges and the developmentally disabled. United Association of Community and Junior Colleges, Washington, D.C.

Roos, P. 1970. Evolutionary changes of the residential facility. In: A. Baumeister and E. C. Butterfield (eds.), Residential Facilities for the Mentally Retarded, pp. 29–58. Aldine Publishing Company, Chicago.

Seevers, C. J. 1975a. A developmental model paradigm for evaluation and decision making. In: H. J. Schroeder (ed.), Agency Self-Evaluation in the Community, pp. 35–36. Developmental Training Center, Indiana University, Bloomington.

Seevers, C. J. 1975b. Recycling-Deinstitutionalization-Local. Paper delivered at the Executive Training Institute, February, University of Wisconsin, Madison.

Seevers, C. J. 1975c. Program assessment chart. In: H. Schroeder (ed.), Agency Self-Evaluation in the Community, pp. 31–36. Proceedings from the Workshop, Developmental Training Center, Indiana University, Bloomington.

Spaulding, R. W. 1975. A progress report on alternate residential facilities in ten agencies operating "pilot projects." Report to the Indiana Legislative Council, Department of Mental Health, Division on Mental Retardation and Other Developmental Disabilities, December, Indianapolis.

Switzky, E., and Miller, T. L. 1978. The least restrictive alternative. Mental Retardation, pp. 52–54.

Vanier, J. 1972. My Brother and My Sister. Griffin House, Toronto.

Wehbring, K., and Ogren, C. 1976. Community Residences for Mentally Retarded Persons. National Association for Retarded Citizens, Arlington, Tex.

Wolfensberger, W. 1972. Principles of Normalization in Human Services. National Institute on Mental Retardation, Toronto.

Wolfensberger, W., and Glenn, L. 1975. PASS—A Program Analysis of Service Systems Handbook. National Institute on Mental Retardation, Toronto.

4

ESTABLISHING PROGRAMS AND SERVICES IN AN ACCOUNTABLE SYSTEM

Brian R. Lensink

Some of the most challenging and important tasks facing professionals and others concerned about the mentally retarded are the development and implementation of programs and services that will meet their clients' individual needs, and delivery systems that work, are accountable, and can change with the times. To date, only a few effective service delivery systems have been developed, particularly at the state level. This chapter provides the reader with some ideas that can be used to facilitate the development of effective service delivery systems.

The basic components of a service system are reviewed, including the ideology, the program components, the systems components, and a number of accountability mechanisms. A specific approach is not suggested since each state or community has its own environment for the establishment of a system. Regardless of the approach used, however, the components discussed must be incorporated to make the system work well.

IDEOLOGY OF A SERVICE SYSTEM

After 11 years of experience in the development of community-based mental retardation services, and after visiting many service delivery systems in the United States and Sweden, one factor has been found to prevail more than any other in those systems that appear to be operating well and that are viewed by constituents and providers as being successful.

That overriding factor is a well-developed and consistently used ideology or philosophical base that underlies the total service system, including its implementation, its staff, and its direction. A strong underlying ideology not only gives the staff a base from which to be creative and innovative, but also provides a footing to which they can adhere in times of stress, adversity, tragedy, or excessive work. The ideology should be the first component examined when evaluating or reviewing a service delivery system or an individual mental retardation program or service, because it is from this base that all decisions are made.

A popular ideology is the concept of normalization (Nirje, 1969), which has strongly spurred the current renaissance of community-based services, including community-based residential services, for mentally retarded citizens in the United States. Unfortunately, many people have chosen to expend their energies in a terminology battle over the word *normalization*. In most cases when this has occurred, more time has been spent arguing philosophically over the meaning of normalization than grasping the major principles of that philosophy and putting them to work in a meaningful service delivery system. The major components of this ideology (Figure 1) include the developmental model, specialization of services, continuity of services, community integration, and statewide dispersal. This section discusses each of these five basic principles, which can serve as the underlying principles of the service delivery system.

The Developmental Model

The developmental model (Figure 2) strongly affects the direction in which a service system develops. Based on the developmental model, programs can modify the rate and direction of client behavior change. As a retarded citizen grows and develops, the system must allow more independence and less structured program alternatives.

The sincere belief that each retarded citizen can learn is demonstrated through programs that prepare a retarded citizen for subsequent steps or goals in his individualized program plan (IPP). These programs are designed to facilitate learning and development. The system therefore accommodates growth and development by offering (or by securing within the community) program options that take into account the individual's development by providing less structure, more integration into the community, and more normalized conditions in which to learn, work, and live.

Specialization of Services

Small, specialized facilities and programs enable a system to offer services geared toward meeting individual needs. One residential setting cannot be expected to serve all clients. The moderately retarded

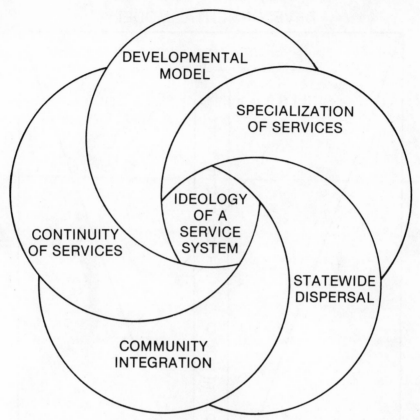

Figure 1.   The ideology of a service system.

person, the retarded individual with compounding medical problems, and the mildly retarded person require different settings and services. Programs can also be specialized according to age, degree of disability, or need for structure. Persons with dissimilar handicaps are not rigidly segregated, but individual needs can, and must, be met within specialized programs.

The principle of specialization is particularly important when considering community-based residential alternatives. Most people in our society sleep, work, and spend leisure time in separate settings—as should retarded citizens. A residence should provide a home environment (e.g., a place to eat, sleep, spend leisure time, relax with friends, entertain, keep one's possessions, and receive telephone calls and mail). Children typically leave their residences during the day to attend public school or other educational programs. Adults generally leave their residences to participate in vocational training or to work in the community. Some

DEVELOPMENTAL MODEL

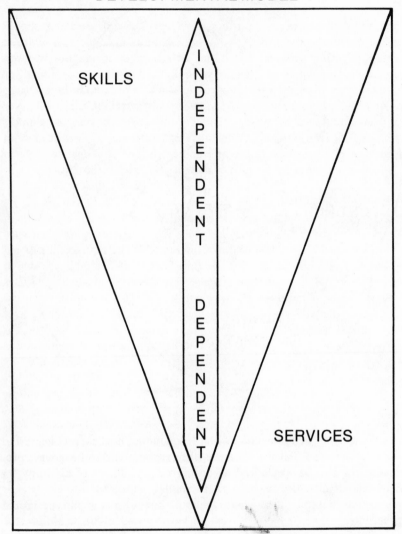

Figure 2.   The developmental model.

leisure time activities should occur at home, as they do for all of us, but many are based in community locations—theaters, restaurants, community gymnasiums, parks, and so on. The division between home and work or school is just as significant for a mentally retarded person as it is for other citizens in our society. Specialization can facilitate this division of function.

Service Continuity

Continuity of programs, a primary objective of a progressive service system, facilitates the growth and development of each mentally retarded person receiving services. Individual development is manifested by a person's movement from a highly structured educational, vocational, or residential environment to a less structured and more normalized setting. A comprehensive system is continually evolving so that services will never be denied because the system cannot provide the program or support necessary for continued development. These efforts toward continuity of service permit retarded citizens, parents, and staff to see what is ahead of them as they work continuously on their developmental program.

Community Integration

Integration of retarded people into the mainstream of society affords them the same rights and opportunities the rest of society enjoys. A service system can facilitate physical integration by constructing typical housing in popular neighborhoods, by locating vocational training centers in industrial or commercial areas, by securing educational services in ways typical for the community, and by ensuring that community resources (e.g., recreational, social, religious, and medical) are available and accessible. Opportunities for interaction between retarded and nonretarded citizens in the community should deepen social integration. Seeking education for children in the same building or classrooms used by other children, securing work training for retarded adults with other workers in the community, and finding a residence with a real family can greatly facilitate social integration. It is important to remember that if the first difficult step of physical integration does not occur it is impossible to develop or foster social integration. True social integration is a learning experience for both the retarded citizen and the community.

Statewide Dispersal

When a new program or facility is being planned, its location is of critical importance. Because a large number of residential facilities could present a neighborhood with more retarded citizens than it might be willing or able to absorb, two or three residences should not be established in the same neighborhood. Of course, a program must be readily accessible to clients and reasonably convenient for the staff. When dispersing programs, planners must thoroughly examine the accessibility of educational, vocational, and developmental programs for those citizens living in the various residential facilities.

All administrative and program decision making must actively consider the preceding five principles and give them high priority in planning and developing community-based systems for mentally retarded citizens. If a strong ideology does not exist and if this ideology is not the basis for program development and decision making, it is questionable, at best, if the rest of the system can be put together effectively and survive.

PROGRAM COMPONENTS OF A SERVICE SYSTEM

The individual services developed for the mentally retarded person are the basis for any service delivery system. Due to the self-contained nature of the traditional institutional approach, many people have a naive view of the extensive network of individual services needed by the retarded citizen. In order to describe some of the more crucial of these services, it is convenient to group them by type. The four service types (Figure 3) discussed in this section include residential, children's, adults', and resource or support services.

In the following description of programs and services, it must be remembered that they can be provided directly or through contract and can be specialized or generic in nature. Most importantly, appropriate programs and services must be available when they are needed, regardless of how they are funded or who provides them.

Residential Services

Residential services are often of major concern in planning a service delivery system. In the past, when speaking and writing about residential types, the author has often attempted to specifically describe from 8 to 15 different residential alternatives for persons of various age groups, functioning levels, and needs. Many people look at these types as the only alternatives and, as a result, limit their own creativity in developing residential settings that can best meet individual needs in their community. For this reason, a new approach is taken here in which a residential continuum that can include an array of alternatives is described. These alternatives can vary in staffing pattern, staff-client ratio, location, size, and program intensity.

In developing a residential continuum, a major effort should be made to provide families with the support they need to keep their mentally retarded son or daughter at home until he or she reaches an age when it is appropriate to live away from the natural home.

In-Home Services   These are a first line of prevention in the residential area and may include: trained sitters for retarded children; parent consultation; training in speech, motor, sensory development, and behavior management; residential respite care; housekeeping assistance; crisis medical and behavior problem assistance teams; trained companions

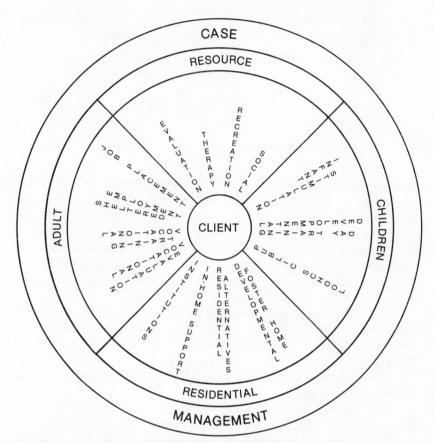

Figure 3.   Individual services for the mentally retarded.

for retarded teens and adults; advocacy and assistance with generic health, education, and welfare agencies; family counseling; behavior therapy and psychotherapy for nonretarded family members; and direct subsidization of costs of caring for the retarded person.

When circumstances prevent a child from remaining with his natural family, or when an adult chooses to leave his parental home, the individual has a right to live in a setting similar to that in which other persons of similar age live. These residential services must be arranged as a continuum of services (Figure 4) that are available throughout a mentally retarded citizen's life.

Developmental Foster Homes   These homes can be described as similar to natural homes, foster homes, and adoptive homes. As is true in adoptive placements, only persons interested in providing a long-term residential service for a child are accepted as foster parents. A

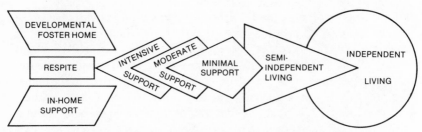

Figure 4.   Residential services for the mentally retarded.

developmental foster home should offer a living situation to a child that encourages a sense of identity and security, which are vital to realizing developmental potential. Children placed in developmental foster homes may come from a natural home, from a state institution for the mentally retarded, or from other child placement agencies. Placements are often made with the expressed objective that a child will remain with his developmental foster family until he reaches adulthood and is, appropriately, ready for more independence.

A developmental foster home should provide a homelike setting for up to three mentally retarded children. The foster home environment should be similar to that of the environments of other children his age living in the community. Also, if there are other children in the family, the child will have an opportunity to interact with, model, and learn from nonretarded children.

A developmental foster home should provide a mentally retarded child with more than a loving family, however. Developmental foster home parents are trained to extend the services of the developmental center or public school program into the home environment. Coordinating with the school program, foster parents are responsible for carrying out the child's specific training program as designated by his teacher.

A Community Residential Alternative   A regular residence in any community that meets zoning requirements and where mentally retarded persons live together constitutes a community residential alternative. The residence may be a house, an apartment, a condominium, a mobile home, or any other type of living environment. It is a place where mentally retarded people have their own room or share a room with another person, each having his own possessions. Similar to any family dwelling, the remainder of the home has living space, kitchen, and baths. It may be modified for physically handicapped individuals by widening doorways, putting ramps up to the doors, or by making other needed modifications.

The mentally retarded persons living in community alternatives attend day programs outside their homes during the week. On weekends they participate in organized community recreation activities, as most families would. Staff members provide care, supervision, and training, as determined by the needs of the mentally retarded resident. For this reason, the staff-resident ratios may vary from residence to residence, depending on the needs of the mentally retarded people living in the home. As a mentally retarded person learns the skills taught in the residence, he may need less intensive residential training and/or supervision. Natural family members are encouraged to visit and participate in the activities of the home, and the residents are encouraged to visit their own natural family as often as this is desired or appropriate. Several levels of residential programming, as described below, can be provided.

Semi-Independent Residences   These residences are designed for adults with successful experience in independent living who are in vocational or educational day programs or are participating in sheltered employment or competitive employment in the community. These adults may have physical impairments or be nonambulatory but have adaptive equipment to compensate for their problems. The person living in a semi-independent situation would generally do his own cooking, cleaning, and laundry, buy basic foods, purchase clothing and personal items, and transport himself to and from work or day programs. Staffing is generally provided through periodic visits by the residential staff, but the staff members usually do not live with the mentally retarded person. Staff members should be available for counseling, providing backup support, and assisting the individual in refining independent living skills.

Minimal Supervision Residences   These residences are designed for children or adults who attend special education or vocational training programs during the day and need experience in independent living. These individuals may also need occasional staff assistance because of physical handicaps while learning independent mobility and physical functioning. Generally, the clients have mastered the majority of self-help skills. Residential staff members provide support and encouragement to the individual as he learns to use public transportation, engage in social relationships, participate in appropriate leisure and recreational activities, and handle basic money management, as well as other community living skills. There may be a need to provide supervision or training in the evening after the day programs, in the morning prior to the day programs, on weekends, and during vacations and holidays. The staff must be trained paraprofessionals who are available on a live-in basis.

Moderate Supervision Residences   These residences are for children and adults of all ages who need assistance and/or training relating to physical handicaps, basic self-help skills, attending to tasks as long as required, or expressive and receptive language problems. Generally, mentally retarded persons receiving moderate supervision learn academic and vocational skills in the day program. They may also require extensive physical therapy, occupational therapy, speech therapy, and sensorimotor stimulation. These services need to be supported in the residence. Staff for such a residence should include trained paraprofessionals and medical and nursing staff consultants. More staff will be required than that required for the minimal supervision residences. The primary staff must be available on a sleep-in basis.

Intensive Training Residences These residences are designed for physically disabled, multiply handicapped, sensory impaired, and severely and profoundly retarded persons, who may require programming and training relative to basic self-help skills and language development. The focus of the program is 24-hour programming coordinated with an off-site daytime special education or adult program. Staffing needs for the intensive training residence are generally quite heavy. The highly trained paraprofessional staff must be complemented by professional technical assistance, consultation, and continuing inservice training. Direct supervision during sleeping hours and intensive support services may be needed within the residential setting.

The Institutional Residence This type of setting needs to be operated as part of the community continuum of services, *not* in competition with other residential options. It is of utmost importance that a good transition be made from the institutional residence to other, usually more community-oriented residential settings. The institutional residence should be made as small and homelike as possible and operated under the total system's ideology, which was discussed previously. The author is *not* suggesting the continued long-term use of this type of residence. Institutional settings should be decreased in size and made as facilitative as possible for those retarded citizens who remain in them over the next several years as these facilities are phased down, and possibly phased out. It should be emphasized, however, that there are major benefits in having the institutional residences administered by, and a part of, the community services delivery system. It should *not* be an independent program.

From the foregoing description of community residential alternatives, it can be seen that day programs also play an important role in the growth and development of mentally retarded persons. As a result, it is essential that an appropriate day program continuum also be developed for both children and adults. These services should be coordinated through the individual program-planning process.

Children's Services

Children's services involve the planning, development, and management of developmental and educational programs for children outside their residences. The range of services might include infant stimulation, developmental day training, and public school programs, including special education. Specifically, these services should provide the following:

Infant Stimulation   These services assist in the development of infants by teaching parents how to provide training in their own home. The service stresses early identification of and intervention with very young retarded children in the areas of cognitive, language, motor, and social adaptive development. If the infant receives appropriate stimulation early in life, the need for more intensive service later may be precluded.

Developmental Day Training   These services provide sensori-motor, cognitive, communicative, social interactional, and behavioral training to preschool children for some portion of the day, in either a segregated or integrated setting. Additionally, this service should assist parents in providing developmental training at home.

Educational Services   These services for children from ages 5 through 21 are the responsibility of the public school system and can be either provided directly or contracted. Coordination between the public school program and the residential setting is essential.

Adults' Services

Services, for adults include the planning, development, and management of day training programs for mentally retarded adults. When an adult client enters the vocational system, typically a comprehensive vocational evaluation is completed to determine the individual's present work ability. A good evaluation can assist in placing the person in the most appropriate service to meet the individual's educational and vocational needs. After the evaluation, a person can be placed in a variety of vocational services including: work adjustment services that provide a treatment and/or training process to assist clients in understanding the meaning, value, and demands of work: job-training services that provide training to individuals to prepare them for specific types of employment; and sheltered employment services that provide remunerative employment to enable individuals to obtain work experience and work at their maximum productivity without extended training demands.

When an individual has the necessary skills to obtain competitive employment, job development and job placement services are provided to assist him in the process. Extended job follow-along is also an important service in order to see that a person remains employed.

Resource Services

Resource services encompass a variety of functions ranging from individual program coordination and follow-up to the provision of specialized services.

Case Management   These services, as mentioned under "Residential Services," are crucial for the coordination of all services delivered to a given individual. This is best accomplished through means of a case management system wherein a single staff member is given responsibility for obtaining all the assessments needed by an individual, for convening all individuals needed to develop a comprehensive program plan, and for providing any needed program support or follow-up to ensure that the plan is successfully implemented, reviewed, and updated.

Casework   These services may be provided to individuals who do not need additional services but who may be living and working independently or attending school in the community.

Evaluation   These services are frequently needed to ascertain the individual's problems and abilities and to assist in the determination of the most appropriate program for the individual. Evaluation services include psychological assessment, physical examinations, speech assessment, and audiological evaluation.

Therapy   These services provided to an individual may include speech therapy, physical therapy, or occupational therapy. They should be provided when assessments indicate the need and should be coordinated with both residential and vocational/educational programs to ensure maximal benefits.

Recreation and Socialization   Recreational programs may also be considered a resource or support service because the activities supplement an individual's residential and vocational/educational program. Recreation does not take the place of day programs, nor does recreation take place during the day program, except as a normal part of the school day for children. Recreation provides the vehicle through which a variety of adjustment and socialization skills can be taught and offers an opportunity to experience a myriad of community services.

DEVELOPING THE SERVICE DELIVERY SYSTEM

After identifying the ideological and program components of the service system, it is necessary to develop the delivery components to make them operational. There are three major delivery components (Figure 5): needs identification and planning, service development and implementation, and program monitoring and evaluation.

Needs Identification and Planning

An accurate and up-to-date picture of service needs is essential. Parents, clients, service providers, and funding sources must work together to assess individuals' needs and determine appropriate service delivery priorities. Determining needs specifically is a difficult process because

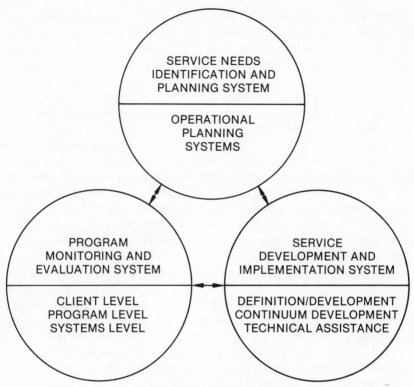

Figure 5.   The major delivery components.

most groups are accustomed to being general in their identification of needs. It is necessary to have accurate projections of the numbers of clients needing each service and the cost of each service so the financial impact can be realistically estimated. It is particularly important to include grass roots participation in the planning process, and thus a method should be developed for encouraging input and allowing these recommendations to be recognized in the outcome. Representation in the planning effort should be from all geographic areas. Feedback on recommendations should be provided quickly to those participating in the planning process.

Service Development and Implementation

After the needed programs and services have been identified and incorporated into the delivery system's operational planning efforts, it is important to provide for the definition, design, implementation, and supervision of each service and program. First, it is important to define specifically the services to be provided. If the services to be provided are not defined, the system may provide or purchase services that are not really needed by the retarded population. After specific definitions have been developed, it is then important to determine how the service will function. This can be done by developing work statements that indicate the size, location, and the specific nature of the service. In social services, there is often a tendency to take whatever is available rather than purchase the services that are most effective in addressing specific needs.

After defining the services and designing the work statements, a procedure should be established for developing service proposals and contracts. This is particularly important when the system purchases services from private organizations within the community. It is crucial that an effective contracting system be developed to ensure that sufficient safeguards exist to guarantee that they are delivered in the manner intended. Service providers must be held accountable for the objectives that have been developed for the mentally retarded person. In addition, they must cooperate and coordinate with other service providers who may also be helping the person. One of the best mechanisms for ensuring this coordination and cooperation is a well-established case management section.

Finally, the area of technical assistance and training must be addressed. Systems have to continually evolve to meet the needs of the retarded person; thus, the system must stay abreast of the rapidly developing and changing technology. New ideas need to be constantly considered by both agency personnel and those under contract to provide services. Openness to change is the key to a system staying current and viable as it develops.

Program Monitoring and Evaluation

The third crucial service delivery component is program monitoring and evaluation. The adoption of uniform, programmatically oriented standards that are well recognized is an important first initiative. The standards of the Accreditation Council for Facilities for Mentally Retarded and Other Developmentally Disabled Persons (1978) have been used nationally, and have proved quite successful.

First, evaluation mechanisms need to be established both internally and externally to the service delivery system. Second, it is the author's opinion that there cannot be too many evaluation or monitoring avenues. Dispersed community-based service delivery systems require many evaluation points and will only prosper from abundant checks and cross-checks.

SERVICE SYSTEM ACCOUNTABILITY

In the previous section, the program monitoring and evaluation process was mentioned as one of the primary service delivery system components.

The emphasis on program monitoring and evaluation has increased dramatically in the last several years as has the competition for limited funding dollars. Program monitoring and evaluation is critical at both the individual client level and on the overall systems level, regardless of the methodology used. It is also beneficial to have multiple avenues available for evaluation, and these should be both internal and external in nature.

Individual Client Program and Evaluation

Clients' programs may be monitored and evaluated in many ways. The following is a description of various alternatives.

The Individualized Program Plan and Case Management   Through the individualized program plan (IPP), which should be developed for each mentally retarded person, a mechanism is formally established for setting specific objectives and measuring progress toward these objectives. Participants in the development of the plan should include the client, his or her family, staff from all agencies serving the client, and the case manager. Since all these persons should meet regularly to assess progress toward objectives, there is an ongoing means by which the quality and effectiveness of services provided to the individual can be assessed. New plans should be developed at least annually and reviewed every 6 months.

The case manager should be in contact with the client's program on an informal basis between meetings for reviewing and updating the IPP. Monitoring of the mentally retarded person's program and the agency providing the services is an ongoing responsibility of the case manager. The basic role of the case manager has been described under "Resource Services."

Coordination with the Day Programs   Since each client in a residential facility should also be attending a program during the day, the staff from this program can act as an external check on the residence. Daily contact will provide a mechanism for assessing progress and discerning problems.

Parent or Advocate Participation   Each client may be visited in the residence by parents, other family members, friends, and/or advocates. National standards require that agencies permit unannounced visits as long as the client's privacy is respected.

Neighborhood Involvement   When homes are located in residential neighborhoods, neighbors serve as unofficial "monitors" of a client's program. The extent to which this monitoring method is effective increases as community involvement and integration increase. What may superficially seem like neighborhood opposition or at least "pesty" neighbors can, in fact, be made into an excellent external monitoring tool.

Overall Program Monitoring and Evaluation

Monitoring and evaluation of the overall residential program can and should be done both internally by staff, clients, boards, and parents and externally by funding bodies, governmental regulatory bodies, advocacy groups, and accreditation agencies. Monitoring and evaluation can be carried out as described below.

Agency Self-Evaluation   Many agencies currently engage in various forms of self-evaluation. It is recommended by national standards that each agency evaluate its performance against its stated goals and objectives at least annually. Self-evaluation, which is carried out by both agency staff and clients, should be documented, and the results should be made available to funding sources and consumer representatives.

Monitoring by the Agency's Human Rights Committee   Each agency should have a human rights committee that includes individuals served and/or their representatives, relevant qualified professionals, and at least one person who is not an agency employee. The function of such a committee should be to ensure that the rights and welfare of individuals served are protected.

Monitoring by the Agency's Board of Directors and/or Advisory Committee   All agencies should have either a board of directors (composed of interested citizens, qualified professionals, and clients and/or their representatives) or an advisory board similarly constituted. The responsibilities of these groups include establishing general direction and policies as well as visiting the program during hours of operation to ensure compliance to established policies and procedures.

Monitoring by Agency Parent Organizations   In addition to a board of directors or advisory committee, some agencies have parent organizations. Whether or not there is a formal parent organization, parents have the right to visit their son or daughter in the program and to observe the program activities.

Ongoing Monitoring by Program Development and Implementation Staff   Programs may also be monitored on an ongoing basis by staff external to the agency who are responsible for the development and implementation of the programs for clients in a given geographic area. For example, if a state has a person assigned to develop services for children in a particular county, this person should regularly monitor all funded services provided to children in that county to ensure that appropriate services are available and are being provided as planned.

External Monitoring and Evaluation by Funding Sources and State Authorities   In some states, annual reviews are conducted to ensure that services are: 1) in compliance with the contractual obligations which would include both programmatic and fiscal stipulations, 2) provided in settings and by means that are of high quality, 3) meeting the needs of the individuals served, and 4) cost beneficial.

Monitoring for Purposes of Licensure and Certification   This monitoring effort should be carried out by local, state, and federal authorities responsible for enforcing licensure or certification requirements. There are generally well-established procedures for this type of monitoring in most states. It is important that the service delivery system staff work to improve these processes and take maximum advantage of their input.

Monitoring by Associations for Retarded Citizens and Other Advocacy Groups   Citizens play an instrumental role in the monitoring and evaluation of programs for mentally retarded persons. As parents and advocates they can become actively involved both formally and informally. In the past, efforts by interested citizens to remedy existing inadequate programs or to develop satisfactory ones have been impaired by a perceived lack of knowledge of what constitutes good programming. Trends are changing, however, as persons who are mentally retarded, their families, and their advocates are becoming more informed about what services are available. They are also becoming more vocal about what they believe should be available.

To assist parents and other interested persons in evaluating existing services, the National Association for Retarded Citizens, under a project entitled "Parent Training in Residential Programming," has developed evaluative materials. A booklet in the series, *Residential Programming for Mentally Retarded Persons*, subtitled "Developmental Programming in the Residential Facility" (National Association for Retarded Citizens, 1972), has been written to help parents become increasingly effective as evaluators.

External Accreditation   Some agencies seek accreditation by a nationally recognized accrediting agency such as the Accreditation Council for Services for Mentally Retarded and Other Developmentally Disabled Persons (a branch of the Joint Commission on Accreditation of Hospitals). Accreditation is a process by which an agency voluntarily seeks the "stamp of approval" of a nationally recognized accreditation body. The service provider or an agreeable funding source pays the accrediting agency a fee for sending a team of surveyors to conduct a review of services based on predetermined criteria. Accreditation, once awarded, must be renewed at least biennially. Accreditation is discontinued if the agency does not maintain and/or improve programs.

COMBINING THE COMPONENTS
FOR EFFECTIVE SERVICE DELIVERY

This chapter has presented the ideology, program components, system components, and accountability mechanisms that need to exist for the development of a community system of services. The real challenge is putting the pieces together into a system that makes sense. Of course, there are many different political, geographic, and administrative environments in which to assemble these components, but regardless of the environment these components are still essential. One should not be led to believe that assembling these components successfully is an easy process. Some environments appear to be so adverse that good systems building seems impossible. Many times the environment has to be changed before an accountable system can be built. This process involves strong advocacy pressure, effective legislative work, strong state executive leadership, and, many times, legal action, as illustrated in other chapters of this volume.

REFERENCES

Accreditation Council for Facilities for Mentally Retarded and Other Developmentally Disabled Persons. 1978. Standards for residential facilities for the mentally retarded. Joint Commission on Accreditation of Hospitals, Chicago.

National Association for Retarded Citizens. 1972. Residential programming for mentally retarded persons: Developmental programming in the residential facility. National Association for Retarded Citizens, Arlington, Tex.

Nirje, B. 1969. The normalization principle and its human management implications. In: R. Kugel and W. Wolfensberger (eds.), Changing Patterns in Residential Services for the Mentally Retarded. President's Committee on Mental Retardation, Washington, D.C.

5
PIECING TOGETHER EXISTING FINANCIAL RESOURCES

Jennifer L. Howse

The funding of community-based residential services for mentally retarded people repeatedly has surfaced as a major obstacle to implementing such services. Yet funds are available, and their skillful application has resulted in some excellent programs. The process is sometimes frustrating and almost always challenging. This chapter presents illustrative approaches to the challenge.

Since New York is one of the more creative states in finding ways to use federal money, it provides an interesting if not downright enlightening example of what can be accomplished.

NEW YORK STATE BACKGROUND

In the notorious Willowbrook case (*New York State Association for Retarded Children, Inc. et al. and Patricia Parisi, et al. plaintiffs* v. *Carey, et al. defendants United States of America,* amicus curiae, 72 Civ. 356, 357 (E.D.N.Y. 1975, 1978)), the Eastern District Federal Court, after lengthy and complicated litigation, ruled in favor of the plaintiffs, and the ensuing decree, signed in April 1975 by Governor Hugh Carey, called for simultaneous institutional reform and implementation of a community placement program for the 5,300 members of the Willowbrook class.

Under the terms of the decree, a "community placement" is defined as follows:

> For purposes of this section, except for placement in hostels currently under construction or development, which in no event shall exceed 15 beds, a "community placement" shall mean a noninstitutional resident in the community in a hostel, half-way house, group home, foster care home, or similar residential facility of 15 or fewer beds for mildly retarded adults, and 10 or fewer beds for all others, coupled with a program element adequate to meet the residents' individual needs (Section V(4)).

Since the signing of the consent order, more than 1,000 members of the Willowbrook class have been placed in the community. Approximately 85% of these individuals are ambulatory, and approximately 60% of them are currently labeled as severely/profoundly retarded. The word "labeled" is used in this context because the clients have shown a tendency to improve after they are placed in the community. Approximately 50% of the clients not yet placed are young adults, and the remainder are younger children and older adults. A September 15, 1978, order of the court established that a minimum of 50 class members should be placed every month into the community. Clearly, resource development has had to proceed at a rather unprecedented rate in New York City to meet these objectives. By co-mingling of local, state, and federal funds, New York is producing a variety of residential settings. The continuum of services in New York City could be considered from the initial vantage point of community-based Intermediate Care Facilities for the Mentally Retarded (ICF/MRs) in a very small and structured setting. ICF/MRs in the community are attractive fiscally to the state, but they are difficult to have certified, because of interagency problems at the state level in rate setting, surveying and billing complications, and the practical difficulties in applying a set of institutionally oriented survey standards to a community setting. For example, the dishwasher water must heat to 180°, which requires electric boosters that can overtax conventional wiring. Fortunately, payment for claims for ICF/MRs can be retroactive to the date of the initial survey, which allows for time to work out interpretative problems.

As of March 1978, there were four ICF/MRs in New York City. These are the most structured and most specialized residences in existence. The disability criteria are the same as those applied in utilization review in the institutional ICF/MRs. The program is cost-based, which is an incentive to agencies to participate, and allows a great deal of staffing flexibility. The average ICF/MR rate is about $70 per day, which is a little less than the per diem cost to maintain the client in an institution.

There are several other prototypes of community residences, each with varying degrees of supervision and training for the clients. There are also family models, such as family care and even a return to natural parents in some cases.

More than 84 community residences and 428 family care homes have been developed in New York City since the signing of the consent decree. The community residences are created through a series of contracts, developed with a voluntary not-for-profit sponsoring agency after a suitable site is found. In New York City, sites include brownstones, single-family dwellings, apartments, and any other setting that is similar to the living situations of normal individuals.

Several different contracts make up each residential service. To begin with, there is a "start-up" or living service contract that consists entirely of state dollars. The living service contract can cover architect's fees, renovations that might be necessary, and furnishings. Two desirable recent additions to the start-up contract provide for a 4-month, full-salaried position for an agency that will commit to develop four or more community residences during the course of a year. This allows the agency to hire staff to find and develop community residences. Also built into the living service contract is a provision whereby staff can be hired a month in advance of the opening of the home. During this time, they can receive special training and can work with clients in their current setting, with parents, and with neighbors.

The second kind of contract is an operating contract, which involves both a federal and a state share. Basically, the client's Supplemental Security Income (SSI) is matched with state dollars. This mechanism generates an annual per client agency income of approximately $9,000 a year, and covers staff and the usual operating costs of a community residence.

This $9,000 a year would support a residential environment where the primary job of the staff is supervising the clients and providing minimal training. It does not provide enough staff for the intensive training and structure that is necessary with more severely disabled clients. Services to such clients entail a supplemental contract. New York state has recently passed legislation known as Chapters 620 and 621 that provides funding for any client who lived in an institution for more than 5 consecutive years. When these clients are moved into the community, their services can be funded through this individual purchase of service entitlement. New York also has purchase of service funds for clients who never lived in an institution but who require special or supplemental services in their community residence.

Mention should also be made of the 202 program in the Department of Housing and Urban Development (HUD) and Developmental Disabilities funds. Funds are now available from HUD for the renovation of housing and for new construction. Of course, new construction is time consuming and involves considerable red tape, so that this avenue may not be appropriate for situations requiring immediate resources. A serious obstacle to use of HUD funds, especially in an urban setting, is the requirement that renovation must include an *entire unit*—whether it is a brownstone or an eight-story apartment. Thus, HUD funds might have the potential of creating large segregated housing situations for the handicapped that make normalized living difficult. Nonetheless, capital federal money is very much needed and desired, in that it can offer states some relief from capital costs that they have been shouldering for community programs.

The Developmental Disabilities program provides an excellent opportunity to fill gaps in services. It is predicated, however, on the presumption that the gaps have been adequately defined by the state. Unfortunately, there are many cases in which these gaps really have not been well defined. As a result, funds are frequently applied to projects on the basis of an agency's effectiveness in lobbying, rather than on the basis of need.

It is recognized that appropriate day programs must be provided to each client placed in the community. The assumption is made that it is the responsibility of the public schools, as defined in P.L. 94-142 (Education for All Handicapped Children Act), to find or create an educational service for anyone who is of school age. Vocational rehabilitation funds and other state and locally funded programs are provided for the balance of adult client needs. However, a gap often remains in providing day treatment, which is a structured individualized habilitative service patterned after the program standards in the ICF/MR regulations. Day treatment is being provided in New York state through a Title XIX service called the Subchapter C program, which is based on the certified ICF/MR status of all state developmental centers (that is, institutions). This program relies on the developmental centers contracting with a provider agency for outpatient Medicaid services. This procedure provides day programs for large numbers of clients who have just been placed outside the institution, as well as for severely disabled individuals who have always lived in the community.

The costs associated with the community residence program must be viewed against the backdrop of institutional costs as a standard of comparison. The operating budget for the New York State Office of Mental Retardation is more than $400 million annually, with more than 90% of that budget devoted to institutional costs. There are currently about 16,000 institutionalized clients, and the state's goal is to reduce that figure to 10,000 by 1982.

The current budget includes approximately $17 million for community residence start-up and operation, $12 million for purchase of service for day and residential programs (Chapter 620 funding), and $8 million for family care.

Institutional costs in New York City range from $25,000 to $35,000 per year and average about $29,000. The costs for community programs, as of October 1977, were:

$8,000–$35,000	range of cost for community resident
$3,500	average for family care
$7,592	average per client per year residential
$4,080	average per client per year day program
$1,536	average per client per year transportation

On balance, the community program is less expensive than institutionalization and offers a higher quality of service. However, when a state is simultaneously maintaining a relatively stable institutional population and developing community-based programs, the total state budget will have to be increased. Generally speaking, the only way to reduce institutional costs is to close entire buildings. In the case of Willowbrook, for example, approximately 100 clients have to be placed in order to close a building. Thus, the initial arguments for developing community programs must be service- and rights-based, not just cost-based, because it takes time to realize cost savings in a deinstitutionalization program.

ANALYSIS OF FUNDING PATTERNS

As stated earlier, at least one of the potential mainstays of New York's community services, the Day Treatment program, is linked to the ICF/MR status of the state's institutions. This situation is the basis for some concern. The institutional ICF/MR program is already massive in many states and shows signs of expanding. These funds have been used by the federal government to carry out institutional reform by offering states healthy financial incentives. The program carries with it the responsibility for a state to comply with standards by a specific point in time or face reduced federal support. The dilemma is that by establishing a heavy state budgetary reliance on federal dollars, 5 years hence (after substantial capital and operating investments have been funneled into institutions) will there be a clear distinction between *institutional reform* and simple *institutional maintenance* with co-mingled state/federal dollars? One of the keys to resolving this dilemma is to substantially redefine through regulation the role of the institution away from long-term residential care and toward short-term, specialized interventions.

There are certain other inherent limits to the use of federal dollars tied to state programs to operate community services. The contract and fiscal accounting requirements are formidable and, by and large, voluntary not-for-profit agencies dislike (with some good reason) the additional paperwork mandated by federal participation. Furthermore, especially with "new programs," such as Day Treatment, there is the question of liability. The federal agents who approve *a priori* a new use of federal funds for a community service are different from the agents who 2 or 3 years into the implementation of a program may decide, *ex post facto,* through an audit that some portion of the state claims will be disallowed. The question then arises as to who is accountable. Clearly, the voluntary agency agreeing to provide a new service believes it should be held harmless. Consequently, the state is usually held liable.

Related to these considerations is the issue of caps and ceilings. The Title XIX (of the Social Security Act of 1971) program, which provides the mentally retarded with new community-based services, is a "runaway" program. These monies are currently open-ended, and states can buy in, constrained only by their available programmatic ingenuity and available match. Many of the same ingredients were present in 1972 when a 2.5 million dollar ceiling was placed on Title XX funds. While imposing this ceiling did stimulate greater use of Title XIX, there is a variable present now that would make the effect of a Title XX cap potentially more devastating. The variable is the trend toward reduced state taxation, as exemplified by California's Proposition 13. This trend is likely to limit the amount of state share available for federal participation.

The moral to the funding story, if indeed there is one, is don't put all your eggs in one basket: diversify your funding sources, and, most importantly, build a strong base of constituency support to insulate programs as much as possible from the winds of fiscal and political change.

SUMMARY

On the one hand, "money isn't everything." To create a responsible, effective program of community services, at least the following ingredients must be present:

Identifiable commitment from state and local executive and legislative leadership

A program of community education to support the installation of community services

An available trained labor pool from which to recruit community service providers and a training capability to keep adding to the pool

An effective constituency group to continually identify problems and assist in their solution

On the other hand, "money talks," and without enough resources, no matter what other elements are in place, there will not be much of a community program. The slings and arrows of legislative fortune, and the problems of federal and state fiscal mix, simply do not override the constitutional entitlements of retarded citizens to equal protection and protection from harm, and to all of the affirmative actions the courts have interpreted these entitlements to mean.

Advocates should certainly make Herculean efforts to work within the system by means of any and all legislative and executive processes. But when reasonable people agree that all reasonable efforts have failed to generate the resources and commitments necessary to provide properly for retarded citizens, more drastic action is called for, or, in more blunt terms, if you can't woo them, sue them.

6

REACHING FOR THE LAST STRAW

James R. Wilson, Jr.

The 1970s were marked by a number of landmark legal decisions in favor of handicapped people, starting with important court tests in Pennsylvania and Alabama in 1972 (*Pennsylvania Association for Retarded Children* v. *Commonwealth of Pennsylvania,* 343 F. Supp. 279 (E.D. Pa. 1972), and *Wyatt* v. *Stickney,* 344 F. Supp. 387 (M.D. Ala. 1972)). Rights to education, habilitation, treatment, employment, and other claims were asserted by aggressive plaintiffs and confirmed by the courts.

Today, litigation is being employed rather successfully by Associations for Retarded Citizens (ARCs) as one of several modes of change. As president of the Pennsylvania Association for Retarded Citizens (PARC) in 1970 and 1971, the author was deeply involved in one of the early and successful ARC class action suits—the PARC right to education effort (*Pennsylvania Association for Retarded Children* v. *Commonwealth of Pennsylvania,* 343 F. Supp. 279 (E.D. Pa. 1972)), which developed out of the association's concern for the residents of what was then the Pennhurst State School and Hospital. This landmark case clearly illustrates an ARC "reaching for the last straw."

The roots of the Pennsylvania case can be traced to the *Brown* v. *Board of Education,* 347 U.S. 483, 493 (1954), decision of the United States Supreme Court. A few years later, in Pennsylvania during the late 1960s, the state ARC began to direct its attention to Pennhurst, a large state residential institution located a few miles outside Philadelphia. As a result of increasing concerns for the welfare of the facility's residents, ARC undertook investigations, media exposés, legislative hearings, meetings with the governor, and other tactics, all to no avail.

So the stage was set, and 17 years after the landmark 1954 *Brown* decision, the time was right for the extension of the *Brown* principle to retarded school-age youngsters. In May 1970 the PARC membership voted to "reach for the last straw"; that is, to mount legal action to address the Pennhurst issues.

Since the focus of concern was a state institution, the approach of choice might have been appeal to the concept of right to treatment. However, PARC's counsel, Thomas Gilhool, suggested that an approach through education " ... lends itself more readily to a class action ... and given the hospitality of the courts, to reaching some of the same ground more directly and more certainly" (Report of Counsel on Possible Litigation Arising from Pennhurst Study, PARC Board of Directors Meeting, Nov. 15, 1969). PARC bought this recommendation, and the class action was launched in 1971 in United States District Court in Philadelphia.

The rest is history; the consent decree that followed required that the Commonwealth of Pennsylvania search out and find all children requiring special education, wherever they may be, and provide educational services appropriate to their needs. Implementation in Pennsylvania followed swiftly, with PARC taking the lead. Members of the state association learned rather quickly that hard work lay ahead.

The impact of the court-approved consent decree was immediate in other parts of the country, as similar litigation was triggered in other states. A few years later, due in no small measure to the efforts of the ARC, Congress enacted P.L. 94-142, the Education for All Handicapped Children Act of 1975 (89 Stat. 781). This major legislation is currently causing a revolution in education. At the least, it will make educational opportunity a reality for handicapped children. It is hoped that it will go beyond this level to make schools healthier learning environments for all children.

The dramatic successes of class action litigation on behalf of mentally retarded persons during the past years may seduce advocates into adopting litigation prematurely or inappropriately. However, litigation is not a panacea, and careful consideration is necessary before "reaching for the last straw."

As a prime requirement to undertaking litigation, there must be good and sufficient reason for such action. It is useful, therefore, to raise some fundamental questions. For example, is there evidence of violations of basic rights, including basic constitutional guarantees, of specific federal or state statutes and/or common case law? Are there serious discrepancies in philosophy, values, and/or goals between plaintiffs and defendants? Thus, defendants might hold the belief that severely and profoundly retarded persons are incapable of benefiting from education or community living. It is interesting to note in this regard that in the early education cases, the basic assertion of fact— namely, that all retarded school-age children, regardless of label, could benefit from education and training—had to be accepted by the courts.

Another illustration of a discrepancy in philosophy that was common in the early right to treatment cases relates to the stance by some defendants that "treatment" should be provided only to persons who have potential for "rehabilitation."

Another reason for considering litigation is failure by defendants to implement stated plans, leading to a discrepancy between alleged goals and actual accomplishments. Frequently, defendants justify these discrepancies on the basis of lack of adequate resources, expertise, or funding. Violation of time lines is a major failure in translating plans into action. In fact, the most common cause for litigation today may be the growing impatience of plaintiffs when plans fail to materialize and objectives are repeatedly postponed.

In short, violations of basic rights, serious discrepancies in philosophy, and failure to implement stated plans and time lines are usually good and sufficient reasons for considering litigation. There are several options, however, other than litigation that are available for bringing about change. Indeed, litigation is usually considered "the last straw."

ALTERNATIVES TO LITIGATION

The initial approach to resolve a problem, of course, should usually be direct confrontation with the person charged with the actual delivery of services or specific programs. For example, a parent might confront the teacher of his child's class or the person in charge of the living unit in a residential setting where his child is housed. Then, if demands are unmet at the direct service level, they can be appealed up the administrative chain to the supervisor, unit director, program director, superintendent, regional director, commissioner of the state agency, and, eventually, the governor.

Another approach is to appeal administrative decisions to established monitoring/advocacy bodies, such as human rights advocacy committees, ombudsmen, professional advisory boards, or state protection and advocacy (P&A) systems. In some states such entities are now well established and functioning, whereas in others they are relatively ineffectual.

Appeal to governmental bodies is another approach that can sometimes lead to the desired change. These bodies might include MH/MR community boards, county commissioners, or state legislatures. Such elected officials are at times more responsive to demands than bureaucracies.

Another alternative to litigation is to reach an agreement with the would-be plaintiffs to create an impartial monitoring/advocacy structure, such as a human rights advocacy committee or a committee on legal and ethical practices. This body can then be empowered with monitoring the implementation of a mutually agreed upon plan.

ADVANTAGES OF LITIGATION

Litigation, then, is only one of several avenues for fostering change. It is generally considered to be "the last straw," adopted only after all other avenues have been exhausted. Yet litigation has important potential advantages, including the following:

Litigation can act as a catalyst for change, providing leverage and ensuring implementation of plans and objectives. It can greatly expedite the rate of change, particularly by establishing firm time lines.

Litigation may be successful in eradicating destructive conditions by, for example, replacing inadequate staff or eliminating specific practices. In addition, it can help to clarify actual conditions through the legal process of discovery. The very process of investigating conditions sometimes helps to improve them.

The threat of litigation may generate "preventive" and cooperative efforts through administrative action, such as the creation of independent review bodies, the establishment of monitoring procedures, or the redeployment of staff.

Litigation, or even its threat, may also generate and/or support legislative action. For instance, many states enacted zero reject education laws subsequent to the early class action suits in the area of education. Likewise, legislatures may escalate appropriations to avoid pending litigation.

Some litigation has precedential value and can thereby have broad implications.

DISADVANTAGES OF LITIGATION

It is clear, then, that not only does litigation have the function of securing a particular result, but it can also help display facts and conditions before the public and decision makers and redefine the questions that must be answered by both. On the other hand, litigation also entails potential disadvantages, including the following:

Any lawsuit entails the risk of losing, which, particularly if it is precedent setting, can lead to regression, decreased leverage, and demoralization.

Litigation can interfere with the implementation of programs. Frequently, institutional staff complain of devoting considerable time for prepa-

ration for litigation, including depositions and preparation of testimony. As a result, they have less time available to implement
programs and deliver services.

In some cases, litigation can lead to delay in implementing change when
plans remain in limbo until the case is decided.

Litigation can produce fragmentation among advocates, often leading to
extreme dogmatic positions. This phenomenon has become increasingly evident within the ARC movement. In some cases, units that
have participated in suits have undergone internal rifts that have
taken years to heal.

Litigation tends to foster an adversary posture, thereby potentially turn-
ing friends into enemies. Even after successful litigation, plaintiffs
and defendants often will need to continue working together.

Litigation can be expensive in terms of requiring heavy commitments of
time, expertise, and money.

Litigation may shift programmatic responsibility from mental retardation professionals to those possessing legal expertise. For example,
a court-appointed master may assume responsibility for program
implementation, or program standards may be developed by an
attorney.

INITIATING LITIGATION

Before initiating litigation, it is essential to obtain the basic information
necessary for making the series of "go—no-go" decisions preliminary to
the filing of any legal action. A systematic approach is desirable, using
a modification of the Program Evaluation and Review Technique (PERT)
model. Key steps in developing information on the basis of which a
"go—no-go" decision can be made include:

Assess current conditions and carefully document the present status of
the situation. More specifically, determine whether the timing is appropriate.

Determine the degree of discrepancy between the existing and desirable
conditions.

Evaluate whether the observed discrepancy represents the basis for a
valid legal issue. For instance, assess whether there is a clear violation of rights and/or statutes.

Define the specific legal strategy and tactics to be used as the basis for
litigation. For instance, answers are needed to such questions as:
What is the appropriate court? How is the complaint to be framed?
What legal precedents are involved? What information should be
gathered? What expert witnesses should be enlisted? How are these
witnesses to be used? What role does negotiation play?

Obtain cost and time estimates on the basis of which to establish a tentative budget and time line.

Identify and obtain the commitment of specific plaintiffs in order to meet legal requirements for a class action, if such is the intent of the litigation.

Select and obtain the commitment of specific amici, if judged desirable, and of expert witnesses. Carefully reach agreement with experts on the purpose and foci of their testimony and on their participation in the discovery process.

Based on the information gathered as a result of the activities outlined above, a final decision to litigate can be made, taking the following into consideration:

Of utmost importance is the necessity to obtain consultation from a variety of people and groups, including program professionals, administrators, advocacy groups, attorneys with appropriate experience, legal centers, and volunteers, including parents and clients themselves.

The specific goals and objectives to be met by the litigation must be carefully evaluated so as to clarify exactly what is to be accomplished, when, and by whom.

Alternative courses of action that have already been pursued must be reviewed, as well as options that might be followed in the future, and the potential results of each must be carefully assessed.

The cost-budget implications of the proposed litigation need to be estimated, including minimum/maximum fiscal projections, win/lose implications, available alternatives, and the probability of success with each.

Once the decision to initiate legal action has been taken, a competent attorney must be chosen. This should be done with the greatest of care. (Parenthetically, it took many weeks to identify the right person to handle the Pennsylvania education case.) In selecting an attorney, a number of factors need to be considered.

First, a personal interest and commitment on the part of the attorney to the basic issues underlying the proposed litigation is an essential ingredient. At the very least, the attorney should have a positive attitude toward retarded people, support consumerism, and be committed to the concepts of civil and human rights. It is helpful if the attorney is familiar with legal and programmatic issues involved with the litigation being considered. He should possess a flexibility of approach so that he is willing and able to negotiate, to develop consent agreements, and to explore other alternatives. Finally, the attorney should be comfortable working as a part of a team involving expert witnesses, other attorneys, legal centers, and consumer representatives, including ARC leadership and clients themselves.

CONCLUSION

There is no doubt that litigation has been extremely helpful in catalyzing change benefiting mentally retarded people. Consumers owe a great deal of gratitude to a select group of attorneys for their help in defining critical issues, raising the right questions, and securing extraordinary results.

It is essential that leaders in the mental retardation consumer movement recognize that litigation is only a tool; decisions on whether or not to litigate must, in the final analysis, be subservient to meeting the basic human values that have always been the focus of the ARC movement.

7

THE IMPACT OF COURT ACTIONS ON RECENT TRENDS IN SERVICE DELIVERY

Richard C. Scheerenberger

It is extremely difficult today to determine precisely, or even to approximate, the full impact of federal court decisions upon programs and facilities for mentally retarded persons. This is true for several reasons. First, we are still too close in time to assess effectively the ramifications of court actions because most of the critical decisions have been reached only since 1972. Second, highly relevant court decisions are still being rendered, and each set of judgments to some degree tends to modify its predecessors. Third, the decisions reached have been extremely pervasive, affecting innumerable state laws and federal regulations. Therefore, the present discussion is limited to reviewing several key decisions as they affect the rights of mentally retarded persons, the implications of these decisions, and some general indications of their impact and associated problems.

KEY COURT DECISIONS

For purposes of discussion, the key court decisions are grouped according to three main categories: 1) due process, 2) programming and services, and 3) involuntary servitude, or peonage. While most of the decisions cited were concerned specifically with large public residential facilities for mentally retarded persons, it should become clear that ultimately their greatest impact will be on community services.

Due Process

Although the U.S. Supreme Court has been hesitant to address the question of constitutional rights to treatment for mentally retarded persons, and has specifically indicated that it will not be bound by lower federal courts, the rights of the mentally retarded to all processes and procedures associated with due process have been reaffirmed. [1]

Most constitutional authorities readily contend that the due process of law clause reflects both procedural and substantive rights. Schwindler (1974), for example, notes that the fundamental objective of the due process of law clause "is to safeguard the individual and his well-being— i.e., his life, his independence of action, and his possessions." Thus, the substantive dimension of the due process clause implies that each citizen, regardless of intelligence, has the right to live in the least restrictive environment and to participate in the mainstream of society to the fullest degree possible. If, for some reason, that fundamental right is to be denied, then the person in question including the mentally retarded individual, has:

1. The right to at least an independent hearing, and frequently to a full-jury trial
2. The right to participate fully in the decision-making process whenever possible, or to be appropriately represented by a parent, guardian, and/or legal counsel
3. The right to appeal
4. The right not to be institutionalized unless he is deemed dangerous to others or to himself

If it has been duly determined that a mentally retarded person requires some form of specialized attention that will separate him from the mainstream of activity, then any programs necessary to modify or correct the presenting problem must be readily available, and the previously enumerated rights should continue to be in effect for the duration of that special service. These two aspects have had a significant

---

[1] Justice Burger, in *O'Connor* v. *Donaldson* (Supreme Court of the U.S., No. 74-8, pp. 3, 11-12, June 26, 1975) made the following observations: "As the Court points out ... the District Court instructed the jury in part that 'a person who is involuntarily civilly committed to a mental hospital does have a *constitutional* right to receive such treatment as will give him a realistic opportunity to be cured,' (emphasis added) and the Court of Appeals unequivocally approved this phrase, standing alone, as a correct statement of law. The Court's (i.e., Supreme) opinion plainly gives no approval to that holding and makes clear that it binds neither the parties to this case nor the courts of the Fifth Circuit. ... Moreover, in light of its importance for future litigation in this area, it should be emphasized that the Court of Appeals' analysis has no basis in the decisions of this Court." (pp. 11-12).

impact upon both programs for and procedures involving mentally retarded persons.

The implications of the due process dimension of civil rights are formidable and challenging, and are all too often ignored by parents, professionals, government, and the courts.

The substantive aspects of due process are of greatest import. They clearly declare that mentally retarded persons should enjoy the privileges and responsibilities of full citizenship and should have their needs met in an open community, except in extreme circumstances. No longer, for example, should mentally retarded children or adults be placed in a state residential facility because of family rejection or inability to cope with the problems of living, the absence of appropriate educational programs, the lack of employment opportunities, or fear of sexual involvement, or simply because they are physically different, slow, or demonstrate peculiar mannerisms. Community alternatives must be created because, as unequivocally stated by the Supreme Court, "Mere public intolerance or animosity cannot constitutionally justify the deprivation of a person's physical liberty" (*O'Connor* v. *Donaldson,* 1975).

Determining Eligibility   While court decisions in the area of civil rights have heralded a new day for mentally retarded persons in protecting their rights to live in a free and open society, they have, at the same time, raised a major question: "Who may be extruded from the community and under what circumstances?" In other words, who may be served in a state residential facility? Early court decisions (i.e., those rendered prior to December 1977) did set forth certain restrictions:

No borderline or mildly retarded person shall be a resident of the institution (*Wyatt* v. *Stickney,* Civil Action No. 3195-N, U.S. District Court, Middle District of Alabama, North Division, pp. 2–3, 1972).

No person classified as borderline, mildly, or moderately retarded according to the standards of classification at Cambridge shall be admitted unless that person suffers from psychiatric or emotional disorders in addition to his retardation ... (*Welsch* v. *Likens,* Civil Action No. 451, U.S. District Court, District of Minnesota, Fourth Division, p. 4, 1974).

No person shall be admitted unless he is "dangerous to himself or others" (*Lessard* v. *Schmidt,* Civil Action No. 71-C-602, U.S. District Court, Eastern District of Wisconsin, p. 4, 1973).

Both the *Wyatt* and the *Welsch* decisions also emphasized that no person should be admitted to an institution when services and programs were available in the community unless the facility constituted the least restrictive habilitation setting.

More recently, U.S. District Court Judge Raymond J. Broderick challenged the very role of large state institutions when he found that

... the principles of equal protection prohibit segregation of the retarded in an isolated clearly separate and not equal facility such as Pennhurst where habilitation does not measure up to minimally adequate standards. More-over ... under Section 504 of the Rehabilitation Act of 1973 unnecessarily separate services are discriminatory and unlawful (*Halderman* v. *Pennhurst State School and Hospital, et al.,* Civil Action No. 74-1345, U.S. District Court for the Eastern District of Pennsylvania, p. 2, 1978a; p. 2, 1978b).[2]

The numerous qualifiers in Judge Broderick's decision make it difficult to determine whether his judgment is reflective of all or just certain types of residential facilities and programs (or the absence thereof). Nevertheless, this interpretation of Section 504 is unique, and certainly strengthens the position of those who advocate for expanded community services and the possible demise of institutions, or at least of their current models.

Since several of these judgments have been on the books since 1972, one would naturally expect to see a proliferation of integrated community services, the effectiveness of which would be partially reflected in a significant decrease in the number of moderately and mildly retarded persons admitted to a residential facility. Unfortunately, available data do not substantiate this expectancy.

The admission pattern has remained relatively constant over the past 5 years. For example, as reported by 269 public residential facilities for fiscal year 1976–1977, 25.6% of new admissions were mildly retarded persons of all ages, and 22.4% were moderately retarded persons of all ages. Furthermore, 49% of all readmissions were moderately or mildly retarded individuals (Scheerenberger, 1978). Thus, despite the posture taken by the courts with regard to residential placements, admission patterns and trends remain the same.

Community Protection   The concept of "dangerous to self or to others" has also produced several serious problems. Many persons believed, perhaps naively, that this concept would refer primarily to the protective placement of the most severely affected mentally retarded person who, without professionally sophisticated support and attention, would fail to thrive or develop. In other words, the anticipated emphasis was to be on "dangerous to self" rather than "dangerous to others." Yet, in some states a growing number of mildly retarded and culturally deprived persons seemingly are being committed to public residential facilities by the courts under this provision simply because they are public nuisances or present some form of disruptive behavior. Thus the

---

[2] Section 504 provides that "No otherwise qualified handicapped individual shall, solely by reason of his handicap, be excluded from the participation in, be denied the benefits of, or be subjected to discrimination under any program or activity receiving federal financial assistance."

"moral imbecile" seems to be with us once again; and, in several instances, admission patterns are reminiscent of the 1930s and 1940s. Like so many terms contained in federal court judgments, "dangerous to others" requires clarification and limitation.

"Voluntary" Commitment With the increasing emphasis upon due process in terms of its procedural aspects, one also would anticipate that an increasing number of mentally retarded persons would be committed on an involuntary rather than voluntary basis. Again, however, the evidence indicates that no appreciable change has occurred in this regard. As reported in 1976, 92% of adults admitted to public residential facilities for the mentally retarded were "voluntary," which, as poignantly noted by Judge Broderick, is an illusory concept (Scheerenberger, 1976).

In reality, the courts historically have had a major role in admissions to residential facilities and have been quite negligent in that responsibility. Although the gross inadequacies of the courts as described by Levy (1965) occurred prior to the onset of relevant federal court decisions, it is still apparent that in many areas the judicial review of the legal status of mentally retarded persons is perfunctory at best. This is well illustrated by the recently initiated appeal by the Michigan Association for Retarded Citizens, which contends that a probate judge did not fully exercise the duties of his position when he held guardianship hearings for more than 100 mentally retarded residents in the span of 75 minutes (*Michigan Association for Retarded Citizens, et al.* v. *Wayne County Probate Judge*, No. 77-535, Michigan, 1977).

Return to the Community Also related to the question of due process is the right of the person to be returned to the community as soon as he no longer requires specialized services in a residential facility. Thus, one would anticipate that this fundamental right to be returned to the community would be satisfied under all circumstances. Again, however, the evidence indicates that this is not the case. In 1976, 67% of the 143 responding public residential facilities indicated that a minor resident would be retained in the institution, regardless of his readiness to return to the community, if the parents objected to an alternative placement. Similarly, 47% of the facilities would retain an adult if the parents objected to placement (Scheerenberger, 1976).[3] Thus, it would appear that in practice a mentally retarded person's rights still remain subservient to the interests of others.

---

[3]This highly questionable position also appears to be supported by the federal government, since one of the provisions of the Title XIX regulations is that when considering transfer to another facility (e.g., a small community-based Intermediate Care Facility for the Mentally Retarded (ICF/MR) the resident and his parent or guardian are to be informed in advance to "obtain their written consent to the transfer" (Section 442.425, C, 2).

The right of mentally retarded persons to live in the community, the right to have their needs met in the community, and the right to have their rights fully respected by all concerned represent the legal and philosophical foundations upon which all other questions of the mentally retarded person's life-style rest. If these essentials are not honored—and not honored in their entirety—then everything else becomes secondary and somewhat superficial (e.g., the right to receive unopened mail is of dubious significance to the resident who should not be in an institution).

Programming and Services

The courts have taken an aggressive role in promoting three programmatic and service areas: 1) education and training, 2) programming in a state-sponsored residential setting, and 3) alternative living arrangements.

Education and Training   The initial landmark cases in the educational area involved Pennsylvania and Washington, D.C. In 1972, a three-judge Federal District Court panel upheld a consent agreement between the Pennsylvania Association for Retarded Children and the Commonwealth of Pennsylvania, guaranteeing every retarded child in the state the right to a free and public education (*PARC* v. *Commonwealth of Pennsylvania*, 343 E. Supp. 279 (E.D. Pa. 1972)). This position was upheld and further expanded by *Mills* v. *The Board of Education* (Civil Action No. 1939-71, U.S. District Court of the District of Columbia, 1972). In essence, the latter judgment contended that no child in Washington, D.C., could be denied a public education because of mental, behavioral, physical, or emotional handicaps or deficiencies.

These two landmark decisions, plus the impact of subsequent court decisions regarding services and programs for mentally retarded persons in residential facilities, have substantially affected educational opportunities and programs in two ways. First, there has been significant broadening of eligibility criteria for public school enrollment. Currently, many school systems throughout the country are offering training opportunities not only for moderately and mildly retarded youngsters 3 to 21 years of age, but for the more severely and profoundly affected as well. It is expected that many schools will soon also provide educational experiences for mentally retarded infants and young children from birth to 3 years of age, regardless of intelligence. Secondly, the nature of the educational opportunities has been substantially influenced by the concept of "least restrictive alternative." Many mildly retarded students and some moderately retarded pupils are being programmed primarily within the environment of the regular classroom with a variety of supplemental support services. "Mainstreaming" has become a primary objective of the educational establishment.

As a consequence of various court decisions, educators must now approach potential special services students circumspectly. No longer is special class placement within the sole purview of the educator or educational administrator. It must now involve an interdisciplinary decision-making process, and any special programming must be authorized by the parents or guardian. If specially placed, an individualized education program (IEP)—a mandate of all court decisions—must be prepared.

It should be noted that many of the provisions of these "right to education" court cases are contained in the Education for All Handicapped Children Act (P.L. 94-142), which mandates full educational opportunities for all handicapped students, ages 3 to 21. This law went into full effect in September 1978.

Residential Programming   The most significant impact of court decisions on life-long programming for mentally retarded persons resulted from those cases involving public residential facilities (e.g., *Wyatt* v. *Stickney* (1972) and *New York State Association, et al.* v. *Rockefeller, et al.* (U.S. District Court, Eastern District of New York, 72 C, 356 and 357 (1973)). In essence, the various right-to-treatment decisions have consistently supported Judge Bazelon's (1979) basic premise that

> the most important fact of the right to treatment is not that the hospital does something for everyone, but that it does the right thing for the right patient. Because individual patients, particularly mental patients, vary so much in their needs, considerable attention must be paid to the patient as an individual.

Thus, in *Wyatt* v. *Stickney* (1972), for example, it was determined that "residents shall have a right to habilitation, including medical treatment, education, and care suited to their needs, regardless of age, degree of retardation, or handicapping conditions." This all-encompassing dictum has had a tremendous impact upon the provision of a wide range of multidisciplinary services to each mentally retarded person in public residential facilities.

To ensure that residential facilities provide proper programming in a suitable environment, several courts have also set forth specific standards, governing nearly all areas of activity, that are to be met by the facilities. These areas include resident living; physical environment; direct care staff, mid-level supervisors and clinical staff; programming and evaluation; personnel recruitment, screening, training, qualifications, and terminations; education; recreation; food and nutrition services; dental services; psychological services; physical therapy services;

speech pathology and audiology services; medical and nursing services; restraints and abuses; resident labor; behavior modification, research and hazardous or experimental treatment; medication; maintenance, safety, and emergency procedures; advisory bodies and volunteers; management; records; and community placement. Most of the related standards have been adopted by federal and state agencies responsible for funding programs for mentally retarded persons both in the open community and the residential setting.

Despite the courts' decisive role in the area of residential reform, it should be noted that most of the residential facilities involved have yet to satisfy the established requirements. For example, in February 1978, the Willowbrook Developmental Center underwent a rather stringent audit in terms of compliance with the 5-year program developed to implement the court's decision of 1975. While Willowbrook had made numerous gains during this 3-year interval, notable deficiencies were recorded in each of the areas of concern, including the rate of deinstitutionalization. Thus, while a court can order, it cannot implement. Even when the state legislature does respond positively, there is no assurance that community alternatives will be established or that dedicated professional and nonprofessional staff can be recruited in sufficient number to serve either in the residential setting or in the community.

Alternative Living Arrangements The early court decisions affecting residential programs and their administration were directed primarily to improving the quality of residential life and clarifying resident rights and related processes. Fortunately, it soon became apparent to the courts that no public residential facility could meet many of its obligations, especially as regards deinstitutionalization, without considerable community support. Thus, in 1975, a consent agreement was reached between New York and the United States District Court, Eastern District of New York, which addresses itself to the problem of alternative residential facilities:

> Defendants shall take all steps necessary to develop and operate a broad range of non-institutional community facilities and programs to meet the needs of Willowbrook's residents and of the class .... To this end, the defendant shall each year for the next five years request the legislature to appropriate additional funds for the development and operation of community facilities and programs to serve the needs of the class. ... Within twelve months of the date of this judgment defendants shall develop and operate or cause to be developed and operated at least 200 new community placements to meet the needs of Willowbrook's residents and of the class. ... Promptly following the date of this judgment, defendants shall request an appropriation of not less than two million dollars ($2,000,000.00) from sums already appropriated by the legislature for the 1975-76 fiscal year (*New*

York State Association for Retarded Citizens et al. v. *Carey et al.,* U.S. District Court, Eastern District of New York, 72 C, 356 and 357, p. 3, 1975.)

In the recent Pennhurst case, Judge Broderick's decision was in marked contrast to all preceding judgments in that no reference was made to improving institutional facilities and programs. Rather, the entire emphasis was on the development of alternative community services:

> Pennhurst as an institution for the retarded is a monumental example of unconstitutionality with respect to the habilitation of the retarded. As such it must be expeditiously replaced with appropriate community based mental retardation programs and facilities designed to meet the individual needs of each class member (*Halderman* v. *Pennhurst State School and Hospital, et al.,* 1978).

As evidenced by Judge Broderick's decision, there has been a gradual but significant movement by the federal courts away from institutional reform to community programming and the development of alternative living arrangements.

Involuntary Servitude

For many years, most, if not all public residential facilities for mentally retarded persons, relied heavily on resident labor. Many jobs, ranging from gardening and maintenance to direct care of younger children, were performed by residents working long hours for little or no pay. This practice ended with the *Souder* v. *Brennan* (Civil Action No. 482-73, U.S. District Court for the District of Columbia, p. 2, 1973) decision which read, "The Secretary of Labor has the duty to implement reasonable enforcement effort of applying the minimum wage and overtime compensation provision of the Fair Labor Standards Act to patient-workers at non-federal institutions for the residential care of the mentally ill and/or mentally retarded. ... " The net effect of this court decision was to establish various classifications of work activity for mentally retarded persons, ensuring them a salary commensurate with their work performance. Although intended initially for mentally retarded persons working in residential facilities, the decision resulted in reasonable wages for all employed mentally retarded persons regardless of where they reside. Although this decision was challenged, the concept was adopted in various federal regulations.

PROBLEMS AND CONCERNS

There is no question that the courts have proved to be a dynamic and positive influence on programming and services for mentally retarded persons. At the same time, the law is a professional field unto itself, and as such, it is neither immune to error nor entirely free of traditions and biases. For example, one major concern is that the principles and procedures of law will take precedence over the needs of the persons affected. Already a number of recorded instances illustrate this danger. For example, one residential facility reported that as a result of court actions, residents 18 years of age and older who had not been declared mentally incompetent had to be released immediately. Consequently, they were put "on the streets with no money in their pockets, no place to stay, and no prospects for employment" (Friedman, 1975).

Similarly, in an effort to realize legal mandates concerning a resident's right to consent, one state declared that a resident has "the right not to be subjected to experimental research without the expressed and informed consent of the patient and of the patient's guardian or next of kin after consultation with independent specialists and the patient's legal counsel" (*Wisconsin Statutes,* Chapter 15.61(j), p. 1056, 1978). As a result of this statute, severely and profoundly retarded residents were denied appropriate medical treatment for severe rumination because a university medical school would not utilize the desired medication unless it was done on an experimental research basis. Since the profoundly retarded resident could not give personal consent, the program had to be suspended. Although it certainly was not the intent of persons preparing the statute to preclude appropriate treatment, it does illustrate the critical need to separate laws affecting the more profoundly and severely retarded from those statutes prepared for the less severely affected as well as from those intended for the mentally ill.

Occasionally, one also gets the impression that if all processes and procedures are observed, the law is content, regardless of the nature of the actual treatment to be applied. Many persons have raised serious questions about the utilization of certain intrusive forms of behavior modification, even though they have been sanctioned by parents or guardians as well as various official review and approval bodies.

Great caution also needs to be exercised to ensure that all aspects of a judgment are monitored carefully. Thus, while the courts have consistently stated that residential services are to be used discriminately and that deinstitutionalization has high priority, it must be recognized that approximately 50% of persons leaving public residential facilities are being transferred to other institutions such as county homes, nursing homes, and state mental hospitals (Scheerenberger, 1978). While it is quite obvious that the courts' expectancies are being realized with regard to deinstitutionalization, the alternative placements are frequently suspect.

As mentally retarded persons become increasingly integrated, at least physically, into the mainstream of society and are given greater control over their own destinies, there must also be the perpetual assurance that their individual needs will not be ignored and that they will not lose the greatest right of all—the right to be themselves, to be mentally retarded.

In essence, the courts have performed their duty by unequivocally declaring the rights of mentally retarded persons to be identical to those of all citizens. Ultimately, however, it will not be the courts that will provide the essential programs and services. Program and service delivery will require what has been always required—a receptive citizenry and a responsive political system.

REFERENCES

Bazelon, D. 1979. Implementing the right to treatment. Univ. of Chicago Law Rev. 36:742–754.

Compliance Report: Willowbrook Development Center. 1978. Willowbrook Review Panel, p. 16. Albany, N.Y.

Friedman, R. 1975. Rights and Wrongs. In: Labor, Litigation and Legal Rights of Residents, pp. 65–76. National Association of Superintendents of Public Residential Facilities for the Mentally Retarded, Madison, Wis.

Levy, R. 1965. Protecting the mentally retarded: An empirical survey and evaluation of the state guardianship in Minnesota. Minn. Law Rev. 5:821–887.

Scheerenberger, R. 1976. Public Residential Services for the Mentally Retarded: 1976. National Association of Superintendents of Public Residential Facilities for the Mentally Retarded, Madison, Wis.

Scheerenberger, R. 1978. Public Residential Services for the Mentally Retarded: 1977. National Association of Superintendents of Public Residential Facilities for the Mentally Retarded, Madison, Wis.

Schwindler, W. 1974. Court and Constitution in the 20th Century. Bobbs-Merrill Company, Inc., Indianapolis.

8

RIGHT TO TREATMENT LITIGATION
Constitutional Theory, Relief, and Preparation

Louis M. Thrasher

The constitutional background of the "right to treatment" litigation concerning institutions for mentally retarded persons centers around the right to liberty. The premise for such litigation, although couched in terms of law-suits against institutions, would be the same in a suit brought against a community service system as long as such a system were operated, or substantially funded, by state or local governmental agencies, and residents were assigned thereto with some element of involuntariness. Other chapters in this volume address the specific legal protections inherent in Section 504 of the Rehabilitation Act of 1973, 29 U.S.C. (Supp. V) 794, and in Public Law 94-142, the Education for All Handicapped Children Act of 1975, 20 U.S.C. (Supp. V) 1401. This chapter focuses specifically on the constitutional due process basis for right to treatment issues, some problems of relief, and some of the practical aspects of preparing for right to treatment litigation.

Juris Doctor, University of Cincinnati; Master in Public Administration, Harvard University. The author is Special Counsel for Litigation, Civil Rights Division, United States Department of Justice. The views expressed herein are those of the author alone and are not offered as the views of the Department of Justice or any of its officials.

CONSTITUTIONAL DUE PROCESS
BASIS FOR RIGHT TO TREATMENT

A right to treatment law-suit places a complicated issue in a forum that is not designed to deal with the issues of how mentally retarded persons should be treated. The professionals in the field are the best qualified to do so. Typically, lawyers and judges are not. Addressing such issues in the crucible of a trial is in many ways like addressing the repair of a fine watch with a meat ax. It is cumbersome, inflexible, lengthy, costly, and emotionally draining, and often it polarizes groups that should be working together. The eventual outcome is never certain. Insofar as the court takes control of a mental retardation system, it tends to remove the responsibility of providing good care and protecting the rights of retarded people from the shoulders of state and local officials where it initially belonged.

In short, litigation is a gamble. Nonetheless, it is clear that conditions can become intolerable, and all other avenues may have been exhausted. It seems that federal litigation is sometimes the only change agent remaining. In such situations, the rights of mentally retarded citizens, who are the least able of all citizens to represent themselves and to bring abuse to the attention of responsible public officials, are too important to be litigated without focusing on the fact that their rights are *constitutional* rights. The right in question is perhaps the most protected of all constitutional rights—personal liberty. Courts are eminently qualified to protect constitutional rights.

The United States Constitution, unlike England's, is a self-contained written document. In practical terms, this means that a basic core of words provides a floor of specific protections for all persons residing within the United States. Thus, the federal and state governments must act so as not to deny any citizen the rights protected by the Constitution. "Rights" can often be granted and denied by legislation, and sometimes by executive discretion, above that "floor" of protection provided by the Constitution, but never below it. No special groups of persons residing within the United States are excluded from the protections of the Constitution.[1] Specifically, there is no exception from the protections of the Constitution for mentally retarded people. The rights guaranteed by the Constitution are personal rights. That is, they attach to each individual and may not be waived by other parties.

The Constitution, adopted in 1789, insofar as it contains limitations on governmental power, is a document primarily designed to limit the power of the central or federal government. It was generally understood

---

[1]Chief Justice Taney's opinion in *Dred Scott* v. *Sandford*, 19 How. (60 U.S.) 393 (1857), since reversed by the Civil War and Amendments Thirteen, Fourteen, and Fifteen, was the only suggestion in United States history to the contrary as to free persons.

that shortly after the adoption of the Constitution, a Bill of Rights would be appended thereto, modeled on the basic rights established by the English experience. Unlike the English experience, our Bill of Rights was engrafted in writing onto the fundamental document establishing the nation. Since the concern of the American colonies that led to the successfully waged Revolutionary War was with the excesses of the English central government, the American Bill of Rights was designed to institutionalize that experience and establish limitations on the powers of the American central or federal government.

Thus, for example, the First Amendment provides that *"Congress shall make no law respecting an establishment of religion, or prohibiting the free exercise thereof; or abridging the freedom of speech, or of the press; or the right of the people peaceably to assemble, and to petition the Government for a redress of grievances"* (emphasis added). The point here is that the Bill of Rights (as used herein, the first eight amendments) was adopted to operate as a restriction on the power of the federal government, *not of the states* (*Barron* v. *City of Baltimore*, 7 Pet. (32 U.S.) 243 (1833)). In this connection, it is important to note that institutions (and community-based service systems) for mentally retarded citizens typically are operated by state and local governments rather than by the federal government.

The Fourteenth Amendment and "Due Process"

It was not until the adoption of the Fourteenth Amendment in 1868, after the Civil War, that American constitutional law, in any substantial way, began to limit the power of state governments to act vis-à-vis their citizens. The long-term constitutional impact of the Civil War (a struggle between the central or federal government and those states that believed that state governments should prevail in certain major areas over the federal government) has been to "nationalize" the Bill of Rights. That is, the course of judicial history for the past 114 years since the end of the Civil War (and as a direct result of the Civil War and the constitutional amendments adopted as a result of the federal government prevailing) has been to consider the protections within the Bill of Rights as they individually arise in litigation. The focus has been on determining whether or not the Fourteenth Amendment incorporates those protections within the meaning of "due process" so as to apply them to citizens as against the power of *state* governments.

In relevant part the Fourteenth Amendment provides: ". . . nor shall any State deprive any person of life, liberty, or property, without due process of law. . . ." It is clear that this language does not restrict the actions of private citizens acting in a private capacity. At first blush this language is straightfoward. However, while the language is written in restrictive terms (i.e., telling the states what they cannot do), by reverse implication it also protects the states in what they can do. Thus, states retain the power to deprive people of life, liberty, or property as long as they do it pursuant to "due process of law." In this regard, there may be no community-based system (although there probably are some) for the mentally retarded that is so devoid of governmental control or contacts as to be "out from under" the Fourteenth Amendment.

It is important to underscore that the Fourteenth Amendment applies to *state* action, not to the actions of private persons acting in private capacities. Unless state involvement can be demonstrated, there is no Fourteenth Amendment case. "Local" governments, for purposes of the Fourteenth Amendment, are considered to be the state because such governments are the creations of the state legislatures and maintain governmental powers at the whim of the state. Of course, governments do not act; officials employed by the governments act on their behalf. Action by such persons is what is controlled by the Fourteenth Amendment. It is also important to note the element of coercion in the word *deprive*. If a person voluntarily gives up his liberty, where is the "deprivation?"

When a state moves to deprive someone of life or liberty, it is normally through *criminal* prosecution rather than through civil litigation. That is, the state is the prosecutor seeking relief for the state from the criminal behavior of one of its citizens. The relief that the state seeks from the court is that the defendant be denied his liberty by being incarcerated.[2] It is clear, therefore, that the states have retained such powers under the Fourteenth Amendment as long as they act pursuant to due process of law—whatever that may mean.

The relevance of this quick brush with constitutional history to the topic of mental retardation is that confining a citizen of the United States in a state institution for the mentally retarded, such as Pennhurst (or any similar institution), is no less a deprivation of liberty than is the state placing a defendant in the "slammer" for having committed a criminal act. True, the avowed purpose of the state in depriving a person of liberty in a state institution for the mentally retarded is not the same as the avowed purpose for confining someone in a penitentiary. However, regardless of the avowed state purpose, it is clear that liberty has been denied. It is equally clear that such action is "state action."

A common factual situation that raises some of these issues occurs when private parties seek to "admit" mentally retarded persons to a state institution. In that situation it is argued that there is no state "commitment," and thus no protections of the Fourteenth Amendment insofar as

---

[2]If the offense is serious enough, the state sometimes asks that the person be deprived of life.

it is a private party rather than the state that is committing the person. Moreover, it is urged that because the "admitting" party is "voluntarily" seeking the admission of someone else, there is no "deprivation," that is, no element of coerciveness.

The response to this argument is twofold. The first approach is based on the premise that the rights in the Constitution are personal rights and that one may not waive the rights of other citizens of the United States. Thus, while the admission of the retarded person is certainly "voluntary" on the part of the person seeking his admission, it certainly is *not* voluntary on the part of the retarded person. Second, it seems clear that the state has acted as soon as it accepts the mentally retarded person as a resident in its institution and is in fact acting to deprive liberty from that time on. Then it continues to make a determination on an ongoing basis as to whether or not to retain the mentally retarded person within the walls of the institution. It seems clear that there is state action as well as a coercive denial of liberty.

Thus, the Fourteenth Amendment applies to this situation and such confinement must be accomplished pursuant to due process of law. The question before the house still remains: whether or not the denial of liberty has been accomplished pursuant to due process of law.

The appropriate point at which to begin an analysis of whether or not due process has been applied in this particular kind of deprivation of liberty (i.e., the holding of a retarded person for treatment) is to note that this procedure has differed substantially from the procedures when a state moves to deprive a person of his liberty because of the alleged commission of a crime. In criminal law a plethora of protections apply when a person is being prosecuted. Thus, in a criminal proceeding, the defendant must receive notice of the charges against him; he must be represented by an attorney; he must have a trial by an impartial jury; he must have a speedy and public trial; he must have the opportunity to confront and cross-examine witnesses against him; he must have a right to compel witnesses to appear; he must be free from cruel and unusual punishment; he must be found guilty beyond a reasonable doubt; and the state must have established before the crime was committed that such behavior constitutes a crime. Based upon the Supreme Court's interpretation of the Fourteenth Amendment over the past 100 years, due process requires these elements when a state is moving to deny a person his liberty for a violation of the state criminal code. Thus, a multitude of protections are automatically accorded one accused of committing a crime, and these protections apply no matter how clear the evidence is against that person.

How about the terms of incarceration in a state penitentiary? The facts in America clearly establish that incarceration for commission of a crime is merely incarceration. Certainly rehabilitative programs are not provided efficaciously in American prisons as they exist today. Due process may not require the provision of rehabilitative programs under these circumstances, since at least one purpose of criminal confinement is punishment. Indeed, the language of the Thirteenth Amendment informs us that "neither slavery nor involuntary servitude, *except as punishment for crime* where the parties shall have been duly convicted, shall exist within the United States ..." (emphasis added).

What happens if the criminal paradigm is applied to the situation in which the state confines mentally retarded citizens to institutions? Typically, the upfront protections outlined above in the criminal process are either not there or are substantially different. Moreover, far from being on trial for the commission of a criminal act, there is no suspicion or accusation of such behavior.[3] Rather, the person is being denied his liberty essentially for having the status of being mentally retarded.

The question remains whether or not a state has a legitimate and constitutionally valid interest in denying mentally retarded persons their liberty for purposes of something other than punishment. If the avowed purpose of confinement of retarded citizens were punishment, then clearly the state would not be acting pursuant to due process of law because there is no crime committed to justify punishment.

The state interest typically expressed in committing and/or retaining previously admitted mentally retarded persons in state mental retardation institutions is that they are unable to care for themselves. The assertion that they might be dangerous to others has generally been dropped as a result of the evidence in the cases to the contrary. Assuming the validity of the contention that each person confined requires care, it seems clear that there is a valid state interest in protecting its citizens who in fact require protection. It is not that the federal Constitution imposes on the state an obligation to protect its mentally retarded citizens who require care; rather, the Constitution *does not prohibit* the provision of care if the state chooses to do so. The question, of course, remains, despite the avowed and facially valid interest on the part of the state in protecting retarded citizens: Is the state justified in choosing to provide care by denying such citizens their constitutionally protected right to liberty through confinement in an institution? The justification often proffered by state governments as to this issue is that retarded persons need to be centralized where they can receive treatment on a planned and evaluated basis; that considerations of economy of size provide fiscal benefits in institutions; and that, at any rate, such persons cannot be cared for in the community.

---

[3]More states are now providing for better protection at the commitment stage as a result of the constitutional litigation starting in the early 1970s. See, e.g., *Stamus and United States* v. *Leonhardt and State of Iowa*, 414 F. Supp. 439 (S.D. Ia. 1976).

Ignoring the question for the moment of whether this kind of confinement is necessary to provide treatment, due process considerations indicate that a state government has a legitimate interest in providing treatment (habilitative care) to its mentally retarded citizens. At least some deprivation of liberty may constitutionally be sustained to accomplish that lawful purpose, if, but only if, it has been appropriately demonstrated on an individualized basis that it is necessary. Furthermore, liberty can be denied only to the degree that its denial is demonstrably necessary on an individual basis.

It is important to remember that the right to liberty is a personal right. It is apparent from the preceding considerations that, if liberty is to be denied for purposes of providing treatment, its denial may be somewhat "open-ended." Under the criminal model, persons convicted of a crime and incarcerated are almost always provided with a term certain; that is, there is a date (or a date that is determinable from the terms of the sentence) on which the confined person knows he will regain his liberty. In the mental retardation area, however, if it is justifiable to incarcerate someone for the purpose of providing needed treatment, then the term of incarceration would logically seem to be a flexible period consistent with the efficacy of the treatment provided and the improvement in the condition of the person that initially led to the deprivation of liberty. A review of state statutes will reveal a power vested in the heads of institutions to release residents (i.e., return their constitutionally protected right to liberty) when (if) their conditions improve sufficiently to reside in the community.

Could it be that a person accused of committing a crime and subsequently convicted has a better protected constitutional right to liberty than does an unaccused, innocent citizen?

If liberty is denied on the premise that it is necessary to do so to provide treatment (and that treatment will improve the condition and make possible the return of liberty), and treatment is not provided, then liberty will never be regained because the condition precedent to regaining it (improvement as a result of treatment) will never be achieved. The result, of course, would be a life sentence without accusation of, or conviction for, the commission of a crime. Not surprisingly, therefore, the federal courts have uniformly held in the right to treatment cases that it would be a violation of due process to confine one for treatment and then not provide it.

In the cases litigated so far the evidence establishes that there has not been improvement in the conditions of individuals receiving the benefits of treatment in institutions. Indeed debilitating conditions in institutions often cause regression. Some argue that such failure to improve justifies continued confinement.

This sounds like a system that is well designed to maintain large numbers of people in state institutions for the mentally retarded. The point here is that, on a constitutional level of analysis, because the right to liberty is a personal right, the purposes for deprivation of liberty must be personalized and the treatment that is supposedly the justification for the denial of the right to liberty must equally be individualized. If the treatment is mass produced, in the sense that everyone receives the same treatment, then it is not treatment at all in the due process sense. It is not well designed to return liberty to the mentally retarded citizens who have been incarcerated for purposes of receiving treatment. Providing a person with someone else's treatment presumably would not be effective (except by extraordinary coincidence) and the condition that led to the initial denial of liberty would continue. The state would then be in a position to continually justify denial of the right to liberty (albeit a justification resulting from its own failure to provide proper individualized care). Therefore, it is clear that treatment must be individualized, that is, geared to the specific needs of the person whose liberty has been denied. Otherwise, the right to liberty has been permanently deprived.

The expert testimony in the right to treatment cases has painted a picture of the professional approach to care of retarded persons that seems precisely to track the legal due process analysis.

Mental retardation is described as a measure of intellectual behavior that is substantially "below" normal intellectual behavior (i.e., that behavior expected of persons in our society at any given chronological age). We "learn" normal behavior in our society by close association with a small unit of people—a family, for example—whose behavior provides a model to follow. When a retarded person is removed from that setting and placed in a new "family" sometimes consisting of 1,000 (or more) members, all of whom have been preselected for acting abnormally, the behavior being modeled is not normal. Therefore, the retarded person in this setting is being taught by his surrounding peers how to behave in an abnormal, or in a retarded, manner. The principle is clear—normal behavior is not learned (by anyone, retarded or not retarded) in abnormal environments.

Obviously, established principles of good professional care and treatment require as normal an environment as is possible, consistent with the needs of the retarded person. In the constitutional sense, this means that retarded citizens improve their conditions by exercising their right to liberty, consistent with their abilities. The evidence to date is clear that state institutions have not met this standard. Based upon the evidence and accepted principles of care, one must seriously consider whether, in principle, institutions will ever be able to do so.

It is a short step, based upon theoretical considerations as well as evidence, to hold that such treatment, if it is to be provided, must be provided in the community.

These considerations lead to the conclusion that what has been generally designated as a right to treatment is not a right to treatment at all. Rather, it is a right to be free from the deprivation of personal liberty without due process of law.

It is vital to emphasize that the theories discussed above are equally applicable to community-based systems and to the old "ship-of-the-line"state institutions—if there is the requisite governmental involvement to establish "state action" and if there is an element of coercive denial of liberty to citizens of the United States.

This discussion has not dealt with the equal protection clause of the Fourteenth Amendment which, as held by Judge Broderick in the *Pennhurst* case (*Halderman* v. *Pennhurst State School and Hospital*, 446 F. Supp. 1295 (E.D. Pa. 1977)), may toll the bell for institutions on a segregation theory. Other chapters address this issue.

The Facts of Institutional Life and
Eighth Amendment "Cruel and Unusual Punishment"

Although the preceding discussion has focused on "law," these trials have largely been based on the presentation of "facts." The facts of life in the institutions have been the real generating engine behind these cases. While the cases have moved on a due process theory, the facts generally have smelled and tasted more like Eighth Amendment "cruel and unusual punishment."[4] This refers to the facts that have been introduced in the public record in all of the cases, revealing extraordinary conditions and treatment of citizens of the United States that have shocked the consciences of federal judges.

Throughout the course of the right to treatment litigation, federal judges appropriately have given great deference to the states and to their responsibility and interest in maintaining control over their own institutions. Typically, the judges sitting in these cases have viewed the merits of the plaintiffs' contentions with great skepticism at the beginning of the trials. One can watch the judge and almost hear a click when the judge, after listening to facts that "sound in" Eighth Amendment cruel and unusual terms, determines that there is something wrong in the institution

---

[4]The Eighth Amendment to the Constitution provides that "Excessive bail shall not be required, nor excessive fines imposed, *nor cruel and unusual punishment inflicted*" (emphasis added). The protection of the Eighth Amendment concerning cruel and unusual punishment have been held to be incorporated into the due process clause of the Fourteenth Amendment. *Louisiana ex rel. Francis* v. *Resweber*, 329 U.S. 459 (1949); *Robinson* v. *California*, 370 U.S. 660 (1962).

and, therefore, his constitutional obligations require him to do something about it. A "remedy" must be fashioned—perhaps good treatment in the institution. Federal judges will bend over backward to avoid interfering with state institutions. However, they have been presented with facts that establish that residents of mental retardation institutions are beaten by staff and other residents, unlawfully placed in solitary confinement (e.g., seclusion), massively overdosed with psychotropic drugs for purposes of control, drowned in their bathtubs because there is not enough staff to watch them, sexually assaulted by staff, tied to their beds, having their teeth pulled without proper care or justification, left for extensive periods in restraints that cause the degeneration of muscle tissues, and so on. Faced with such facts, federal judges at that point in the trials literally have no choice if the Constitution is to have meaning within their districts.

Such facts have existed in the treatment cases to date, and it is interesting to watch the judges move from a position of great skepticism to a position of wonderment then finally to a position of anger over the fact that such conditions exist. When this point is reached, it is clear that their attitude has become one of "something must be done about it." The "something" typically selected by judges is effective and appropriate treatment. The judges at this stage in the trial have viewed treatment more as a remedy to address what has been established by the facts—cruel and unusual punishment. In this sense, the courts have approached the right to treatment issues almost on the basis of holding the states to a Faustian offer of treatment in return for the constitutionally protected right to liberty of the mentally retarded citizens of the United States held in institutions.

Once the judges have reached this stage, they have listened much more attentively and responsively to the witnesses who address the issues of the "least restrictive alternative." This concept has been presented in terms of the premise that better, less costly (Conley, 1973), and less invasive treatment can be provided in the community that in an institution that has been demonstrated to be cruel and, unfortunately, often not so unusual.

This process of change in attitude and approach by the judges often happens during the testimony of the first one or two witnesses. Typically, these witnesses are nationally recognized experts in the treatment of mental retardation. Usually they have toured the institution, interviewed supervisors and employees, reviewed institution records, and evaluated the treatment of residents. Such witnesses do an excellent job of educating the judge regarding mental retardation and its treatment, and they then describe the "parade of horribles" inside the institution. Such testimony typically takes up the first two days of trial. While placed on the stand as "expert witnesses" in the field of mental retardation, they have been used as very effective conduits to place massive amounts of facts in the record, and they have been able to explain the relevancy and meaning of such facts to the court. Typically, as the judge becomes educated, he has "taken over" much of the questioning of these witnesses.

It has been important not to lose the judge of this juncture. Once the judge clears the hurdle of concluding that there is something terribly wrong in the institution and that he must do something about it, it is essential to bring him back to the legal nexus of these lawsuits. That is, personal liberty is at stake. Having now begun to think about how to remedy cruel and unusual conditions, and being reminded that the legal essence of the case is really personal liberty, the judges have then quite easily made the transition from merely ordering that treatment be improved within the institution to seriously considering granting liberty. In the practical sense, this means, of course, that treatment, if required, is to be provided in a setting that is not as restrictive or invasive of personal liberty as is the institution. Again, cautiousness is indicated if the court seems to be addressing liberty only *as a remedy*. Liberty, of course, is a substantive right protected in and of itself by the Constitution. Persons deprived of liberty without due process of law have a right to have their liberty returned to them. A court may not make liberty contingent upon the resources of the state. Fortunately, in this field the evidence at trial has been overwhelming that treatment is much more efficacious in a community setting and, in the long run, less costly.

Thus, the Eighth Amendment type of facts have been what have gained the judges' attention at trial and overcome their reluctance to interfere with state institutions. They have then, during trial, moved to a position of considering ordering better care in the institution as a remedy. After this point has been reached, the emphasis on liberty and its parallelism regarding the appropriate way to train and care for retarded people have moved the judges toward ordering deinstitutionalization. Such an order, of course, implies an appropriate community setting into which institution residents can be moved.[5]

SOME PROBLEMS OF RELIEF

Community programs may not exist or, if existing, may already be filled, so that meaningful relief would require that such settings be created. The

---

[5]It is certainly possible for horrendous conditions and cruel and unusual practices to be replicated in small settings (cf., *Gary W. and the United States* v. *Stewart*, 437 F. Supp. 1209 (E.D. La. 1976)). Thus, a properly operated community system must be "accountable." Community systems have a major advantage over closed institutions with regard to their "openness" and greater likelihood that abuse will be discovered and remedied.

judge could lawfully conclude that the state is not mandated by the Constitution to run a mental retardation system at all, and if it is not willing to run its extant system in a constitutional manner, the system can be ordered closed. No one would benefit from such a Draconian measure, and political reality would lead the state governments to opt to provide a mental retardation system. The courts have, therefore, appropriately ordered community placement and have waited to evaluate the responses of the states. To the surprise of no one, the crunch has come at the relief stages of the treatment cases.

Some states have argued that the federal courts are jurisdictionally barred from ordering the development of community care systems by the Eleventh Amendment. The Eleventh Amendment provides that "the Judicial power of the United States shall not be construed to extend to any suit in law or equity, commenced or prosecuted against one of the United States by Citizens of another State or by Citizens or Subjects of any Foreign State." (See generally Jacobs, 1973.)

The Eleventh Amendment was adopted in 1795, 4 years after the Bill of Rights was ratified, specifically to reverse the holding in one of the first cases to come before the Supreme Court. One of the grants of jurisdiction to the federal judiciary in Article III of the Constitution is "To controversies ... between a State and Citizens of another State. ..." In *Chisholm* v. *Georgia*, 2 Dall. (2 U.S.) 419 (1793), the court held that a citizen of another state or of a foreign country may bring suit against a state in federal court to enforce the contract obligations of the state government. The Supreme Court held that it had jurisdiction and held the state liable. The court seemingly held that the word "controversies" in Article III was not limited to suits otherwise recognizable at common law, because at common law one could not (it was maintained) sue the sovereign.

The language of the amendment is written in diversity jurisdiction language. That is, its specific language applies to lawsuits filed by citizens of another state or of a foreign state against one of the states. The Supreme Court has since held that the amendment, or parallel principles of common law sovereign immunity, bars suits against a state brought in federal court, even by a citizen against his own state, i.e., where there is no diversity of citizenship (*Hans* v. *Louisiana*, 134 U.S. 1 (1890)).

If such a suit as was brought in *Hans* were viable, then plaintiffs could sue their own "sovereign" state in federal court and suits by citizens of other states would remain barred by the terms of the Eleventh Amendment. In deciding *Hans*, the court reconsidered the basic question involved in *Chisholm*. If Article III were no more than a statement that suits could be brought that were otherwise recognizable at common law, then, because sovereign immunity was part of the common law, *Chisholm* had been decided erroneously; states could never be sued, even by their own citizens, without state consent; the Eleventh Amendment eliminated the erroneous ruling of *Chisholm* concerning noncitizen suits; and suits against states, by their own citizens, remained barred by preexisting common law sovereign immunity. However, if Article III were considered an affirmative grant of jurisdiction in derogation of the common law, *Chisholm* was decided correctly; federal question jurisdiction would permit unconsented suits as *Hans*; and the Eleventh Amendment restored sovereign immunity *only* to the diversity cases specified in the Amendment.

The court adopted the former construction and held that the purpose of the Eleventh Amendment had been to ensure incorporation of the entire common law concept of sovereign immunity and that, therefore, the *Hans* suit was barred. Thus, common law sovereign immunity was granted constitutional status emanating from Article III and the Eleventh Amendment.

The *Hans* decision, by whichever headnote it has subsequently been characterized, either Eleventh Amendment or common law sovereign immunity, eliminated the sovereign immunity distinction between the classic diversity cases spelled out in the Eleventh Amendment and suits against a state by its own citizens.

Subsequent interpretations of the amendment have held that, even though the state is not named as a defendant, if the relief is retroactive in nature and impacts substantially upon the state treasury, the relief is barred. However, the court has clearly held that even though there is a monetary impact on the state, if it is "merely ancillary" to implementing the protections of Fourteenth Amendment rights, such relief is not barred by the Eleventh Amendment (*Edelman* v. *Jordan*, 415 U.S. 651 (1974)).[6] One of the key elements determining that costs of relief are "merely ancillary" to protecting Fourteenth Amendment rights is to show that the relief is prospective in nature and not retrospective. Clearly, creating community systems as future residences is prospective relief. Thus, the phrasing of the issues of relief before the court and the way they are cast in trial are very important. Therefore, it must be clearly established in trial that the court is dealing with basic substantive Fourteenth Amendment rights, that they have been seriously impaired, and that what is being sought is prospective relief in support of the Fourteenth Amendment.

There is a basic tension between the Fourteenth Amendment and the Eleventh Amendment. In order to successfully bring a lawsuit under the Fourteenth Amendment, it is necessary to show "state action." The more

---

[6]Nor does the fact that such ancillary costs are high establish the Eleventh Amendment as a bar. See *Milliken* v. *Bradley*, 433 U.S. 267, 289 (1977) ($6 million relief in school desegregation case).

the action of the state is shown (and, therefore, the stronger the suit under the Fourteenth Amendment), the more the awarded relief will be forthcoming from "the state," rather than other sources. A court order will therefore run in that direction, and the possibility of the decision running counter to the protections of the Eleventh Amendment would seem to increase.

The history of the Eleventh Amendment indicates that it is concerned with direct attacks upon state treasuries. In preparing the lawsuit and putting in proof, it is important, therefore, to focus on what monies are already available to the states without further impact upon the state treasury. Thus, within the executive branch of the state there are sums of money appropriated that are not used, or that could be better used to suit both the state purpose reflected in the appropriations bills and the federal purpose in protecting Fourteenth Amendment rights. An order from a court moving such monies from one executive department to another for purposes of enforcing basic constitutional rights may not raise a valid Eleventh Amendment issue.

This may suggest that funds appropriated for providing care and treatment in an institution may be subject to a court order transferring them from the institution to community-based facilities as the population in the institution is reduced and the population in community systems is raised. Thus, conceptually, money that is already appropriated by the state for providing care and treatment for residents of the state institution is being transferred with such residents when they leave the institution. This may be consistent with the state purpose of providing better care and treatment to retarded citizens at a lower cost per capita. As more people leave the institution, more funds that have been appropriated for new construction or for repairs and maintenance of buildings at the institution should be made available as buildings are depopulated. And, as residents leave the institution, more operating funds are freed. As such funds are freed, they would logically be subject to transfer with the residents of the institution to the community. A court order so providing does not present the same issue as does the classic Eleventh Amendment case. Therefore, the repair, maintenance, and construction plans of institutions and their costs of operations are important evidence for providing a basis upon which a court can order appropriate and effective relief.

Of course, the state is capable of waiving its Eleventh Amendment protections. This can be done, *inter alia*, by consenting to be bound by a federal court order and, it would seem, by major state officials subscribing to the terms of a consent decree.

Recent federal legislation may well obviate Eleventh Amendment problems in this area. Section 5 of the Fourteenth Amendment provides:

"The Congress shall have power to enforce, by appropriate legislation, the provisions of this article." This language has been interpreted to mean (despite the language of the Eleventh Amendment) that, if Congress has passed a statute that provides for the liability of a state in federal court for enforcing the Fourteenth Amendment, federal courts have jurisdiction to hear such cases and to order appropriate relief (*Fitzpatrick* v. *Bitzer*, 427 U.S. 445 (1976)). Public Law 94-142 and Section 504 of the Rehabilitation Act of 1973 provide substantial bases for arguing that Congress has acted under Section 5 to enforce the Fourteenth Amendment and that, therefore, even though appropriate relief may substantially impact upon state treasuries, such litigation, and the relief engendered thereby, are not barred by the Eleventh Amendment. Thus, the statutory avenues of litigation are not to be viewed as separate and apart from the constitutional avenue of litigation, but rather as a part of the warp and woof of the lawsuit and the phrasing of the issues so as to enable the court to order appropriate relief.

This discussion of the constitutional theory and the argument most often raised as a defense to implementation of relief has been presented as the necessary basis for formulating the issues so that preparation for trial (i.e., the collection of facts) may proceed in an orderly and productive fashion.

PREPARING FOR RIGHT TO TREATMENT LITIGATION

Lawsuits are won by those parties who are best prepared. Preparation in the context of right to treatment suits translates into facts. Amassing the facts upon which to bring a successful right to treatment suit involves a tremendous amount of hard work and preparation. The best tools for gathering such facts in these cases are depositions, expert tours, and records analysis.

Depositions

Prior to selecting persons to be deposed, substantial groundwork must be accomplished. A history of the institution should be obtained or prepared. To understand what the institution is today, one must understand its past and the plans for its future. All budgets and appropriations bills that bear upon the institution and alternative care systems should be collected. One must obtain, thoroughly analyze, and understand the budget requests submitted by the executive branch of the state to the legislature over a substantial period of time. Typically, such documents contain recitations of inadequacies and a breakdown of funds, by source, needed to correct the deficiencies in the institution. This provides a basis for subsequent depositions in which those who prepared the budget submissions can detail the deficiencies. Those documents will also provide a basis for comparing costs in the institution with costs in the communities.

An organizational diagram of the institution, including functional descriptions of the different subunits, is mandatory. Information should be obtained from interested parents and community groups of important events that have had an impact on the institution and community services to provide the basis for a chronology of key events. Information obtained from depositions can then be compared with this chronology to assess its validity.

After obtaining as much advance information as is reasonably possible, depositions of employees of the institution should be taken. The employees should be subpoenaed to the depositions with appropriate documents. Subpoenaed documents should include such items as notes and minutes of meetings, complaints of mistreatment of residents, notices of deficiencies received from regulating agencies, self-survey forms listing deficiencies for groups such as the Joint Commission on Accreditation of Hospitals, Medicaid reviews, lists of deaths and causes of deaths within the institution, and selected resident files (including both random samples and specific instances of suspected mistreatment). The contents of all such documentation should be thoroughly discussed with the appropriate person in the deposition.

The choice of persons to depose is crucial. Being an outsider to the institution makes that task difficult. Hence, the importance of performing the background work before noticing depositions cannot be under-estimated. Employees at all levels and in all areas of the institution should be deposed. Since the total life-style of the institution is on trial in a right to treatment suit, it must be well documented.

The order of taking depositions should be to start at the bottom of the administrative hierarchy and work up. Therefore, the first persons to be deposed are the direct care staff, and the last person should be the superintendent.

The depositions of the direct care staff who work daily on the living units with the residents should be taken in great detail, so that the exact nature of the daily duties are reflected in the record. After the personal background of the deponent is established, including his education and training for his current job, he should be asked to explain in detail, and in chronological order, his work on a typical day. The records and reports the person typically completes should be thoroughly discussed.

The records and reports prepared by the direct care staff on a day-to-day basis are the real treatment records upon which the institution relies. Typically, such direct care staff will be charged with performing certain basic skills training of the clients, and they are responsible for documenting the daily training on prescribed forms. Those forms have invariably shown that everyone receives the same "treatment," no matter what his needs. Usually, such forms will not be the records that are proffered by the institution as the records upon which they rely. Nevertheless, by the very nature of things, they are the records upon which the personnel delivering the care must rely.

Depositions should be taken of representative direct care staff in every living unit on every floor and on every shift. The institutional routine will often change dramatically from shift to shift, from unit to unit, and from building to building. However, one thing has been clear: such routine changes have little or no relationship to the needs of the residents. Thorough depositions of such direct care staff will reflect that they often have so many housekeeping duties that they cannot possibly be providing any meaningful training and treatment.

An aggressive pursuit of the daily activities of direct care staff usually generates some astounding stories. One example concerns a second floor in a residential dormitory that housed nonambulatory residents. The staff person deposed testified that she worked alone. When she was asked how she would safeguard all the nonambulatory residents in case of fire, it was explained that they would be dropped down a tube that runs out the window and spirals down to the ground below. The far end of the tube at the ground level was closed with a hatch door. The staff person would have to place the first person in the tube and then run down the steps and open the door to remove the resident. Then she would run back up to the second floor and place another resident in the tube. This routine would have to be repeated until everyone was evacuated. Obviously, under such conditions, no fire drills were performed. This is a classic example of what is found everywhere: vastly overburdened staff are at the mercy of "the system" regardless of enormously good intentions.

Other depositions should clearly show that there simply is not enough staff on duty to adequately care for all the residents at any time, but particularly during bath times. When asked on deposition how this problem was dealt with, direct care staff have stated that they left residents alone in their bathwater. As a result, some epileptic residents have drowned. Other direct care staff employees have testified that they have literally tied residents to toilets for long periods of time while the staff went to "toilet" other residents. The impact of such testimony upon a federal court in a civil rights case is, of course, substantial. Here, again, it is important to show that the findings are a result of many people with pressing needs for care being housed together, that is, in an institution.

After the direct care staff have been deposed, depositions should start moving up the administrative hierarchy. The next level of depositions typically would be the cottage or living unit supervisors. These depositions should be based on the knowledge gained in the depositions of the direct care staff. Here, of course, different records will be subpoenaed, and the discrepancies between the real records being maintained by the direct care staff and other records being prepared at the supervisory level will become evident. The depositions at the supervisory level, as well as all others, should be taken in precisely the same way as those of the direct care staff. They should include the detailed recitation of typical daily activities. At each level of depositions, the deponent should specifically be asked to recount every example of injury, brutality, solitary confinement, overdrugging, and so on, that has been witnessed or heard of. Every deponent should be asked what he did with such information, to whom he conveyed reports of such incidents, and the reaction from supervisors to such reports.

The purpose of noticing depositions from the bottom of the management pyramid upward is that the plaintiff should never take a deposition of a supervisory agent of the institution without knowing more about the operation below him than the supervisor knows himself. In this manner, a plaintiff should never receive an answer to a question that surprises him or hurts the case. By the time the deposition of the superintendent of the institution is taken, plaintiff's counsel should know more about day-to-day operations of the institution than does the superintendent. Usually, the superintendent will testify that his policy is such that the practices already established in earlier depositions are not occurring. Counsel taking the deposition is then in a position to ask if such practices did occur, would they be contrary to the policy of the superintendent? The answer, of course, is always yes.

Proceeding in this fashion, invariably the superintendent essentially ends up testifying in favor of the plaintiff during the deposition.

Expert Tours

Expert tours of the institution are excellent opportunities to gather factual evidence. This is an important process because, typically, the judge will have little or no experience with institutions or mentally retarded people. It would be very risky for a plaintiff's case for the judge to tour an institution before trial, because he may erroneously conclude that the behavior of residents he sees in the institution is the reason why they are there. It takes well-prepared expert testimony to educate the judge to a point where he can recognize that the institutional environment is itself the cause of much of the abnormal behavior of the residents. The expert tours, then, should be viewed as the "eyes" of the court. After trial, a personal tour of the facility by the judge may be advisable, provided that he is accompanied by well-qualified experts.

Each expert should tour at varied hours and days and visit all buildings, rooms, and training areas.[7] He should be accompanied by a photographer who takes photographs at the expert's direction. Such photographs are invaluable and provide an excellent basis for well-structured testimony. These photographs furnish an opportunity to explain to the court the impact of institutional practices and procedures and the effects of a nonstimulating environment upon retarded residents. To that end, there must be enough copies of such photographs arranged in "see through" folders in notebooks for the judge to have a copy before him as he follows the testimony.

The expert should view the training of residents with appropriate schedules in his possession so that he can determine whether specifically named residents are in fact receiving training at the time and place specified in the schedules. The expert should interview staff members, including the superintendent, to obtain their explanations of what he has observed, so that it cannot be maintained at trial that "if only the witness had asked us, we would have told him that his facts were erroneous." If institutional personnel refuse to talk to the expert on his tour, he should include that fact in his testimony so that the judge will understand the situation.

As the expert is testifying to lay the foundation for his professional opinions as to whether or not the institution meets minimally acceptable standards of care, he is in truth a "fact" witness. Thus, he relays to the court what he saw and heard at the institution and is in a position to explain the relevancy of all the practices and conditions of institutional life as they affect the residents. He is, therefore, a conduit for placing in the record a massive amount of factual information.

The first witness to take the stand should be an expert in the diagnosis of mental retardation, its "treatment," the design of habilitative programs, and the design and management of habilitative care delivery systems for the mentally retarded. He should be qualified to define mental retardation (and differentiate it from other conditions), describe the developmental process, and explain the advantages of normalized settings and practices. He should also have seen many institutions, toured the institution at issue in the case, and be able to demonstrate from records and observation of individual residents that regression has occurred in the institution.

---

[7]The practice of institutional staff providing VIP tours that stop at only "showcase" points is well known. The author is aware of a tour where the staff placed new clothes on the residents of one ward, removed those clothes after the tour passed, raced ahead with the clothes, and placed them on other residents.

Subsequent expert witnesses should be selected so as to provide some overlapping with each other's areas of expertise, so that the court hears the same message from several experts and does not feel that a minority view is being expressed. Typically, such experts should testify concerning medical care, misuse of drugs, education, vocational training, and community care. It is important to have some experts testify who have toured both the institution and the local community care facilities and who can testify concerning photographic exhibits from both. Very effective testimony from these experts flows naturally from identifying residents in the community who were in the institution for several years. Typically, the institutional file will show that the resident had certain basic life skills at the time of admission which were subsequently lost during the time spent in the institution. The community records will often show that such skills were regained shortly after release from the institution and placement in a well-designed community program. The judge will have no problem understanding the relevance of this kind of evidence.

Records Analysis

The records maintained by the institution are its business records and, therefore, generally are admissible. For the protection of the residents' privacy, an order should be prepared for the judge's signature limiting access to such records to the attorneys of record and their agents. The protective order should also provide that any such records placed in evidence will not reflect the names of the residents.

When analyzed, the resident files will almost always demonstrate a pattern of regression of skills during the period spent in the institution. Summaries of such data should be prepared under the direction of an expert witness and placed in evidence.

Resident files will also demonstrate a pattern or practice of overuse of psychotropic medications and of various kinds of seizure control drugs. These medications, when overused or misused, cause serious permanent damage and should be thoroughly addressed by expert testimony.

There is always a "smoking gun" record in each case. In *Halderman* v. *Pennhurst State School and Hospital*, 446 F. Supp. 1295 (E.D. Pa. 1977), the institutional staff maintained a chart that showed broken bones each month. This record graphed the number of unexplained serious fractures each month for a several-year period. Typical fractures were of backs, pelvises, legs, and arms. After reviewing this record on the stand during trial, the expert, Dr. Philip Roos, when asked how he would characterize the record, testified that "... [T]he thing looks a little like a battlefield report. It appears that it is physically hazardous for the residents to be in the environment."

CONCLUSION

This presentation has not been exhaustive. Indeed, the subject of this chapter could easily fill an entire book. In closing, it should be remembered that principles of care for mental retardation have changed in the past and undoubtedly will change in the future. In the right to treatment litigation, it is important to guarantee the constitutional rights of retarded citizens and to leave a flexibility to accommodate the realities for the future. It is essential to guarantee liberty, as is required by the Constitution, but this should not prevent advancements in appropriate and effective "treatment." Chief Justice Marshall's comment (*Cohens* v. *Virginia*, 6 Wheat (19 U.S.) 264, 387 (1821)) remains pertinent:

> A constitution is framed for ages to come, and is designed to approach immortality as nearly as human institutions can approach it. Its course cannot always be tranquil. It is exposed to storms and tempests.

REFERENCES

Conley, R. 1973. The Economics of Mental Retardation. The Johns Hopkins Press, Baltimore, Md.
Jacobs, C. E. 1973. The Eleventh Amendment and Sovereign Immunity. Green Press, Westport, Conn.

9

ATTITUDINAL, SOCIAL, AND LEGAL BARRIERS TO INTEGRATION

Andrea S. Knight

To the degree that social and legal barriers exist, community residential options for all mentally retarded persons fail to receive needed support. What are these barriers, and how do they affect provision of community services? This chapter deals with some of these major barriers.

The position statements on residential services of the National Association for Retarded Citizens (NARC, 1976) conclude with, "It is the right of handicapped individuals, including mentally retarded persons, to live their lives as normally as possible within the community. Every state and community must give precedence to the establishment of a variety of living arrangements and the necessary support and program services within the community." This statement summarizes the goals for residential services for retarded people.

The NARC has established additional criteria that stress living experiences appropriate to the functioning level and learning needs of the individual as well as access to habilitative programs based on the developmental model of programming. A residential setting should be an integral part of a total program, not just a place to house people. The goal is to provide the best possible quality of programming while encouraging the retarded person to do for himself those things that he is able to do.

Additionally, the courts have ruled that each person's program evaluation should lead to a placement in an environment least restrictive to his liberty, "... living in an ordinary house, attending classes in a regular school building, working ... and taking an active part in regular leisure time activities ... using ordinary segments of the environment such as gyms, school yards, restaurants and public transportation along with the rest of the population" (National Association for Retarded Citizens and The International League of Societies for the Mentally Handicapped, 1976).

Yet a gap appears to exist between these ideals and the reality of some services. This disparity suggests the dangerous barrier of negative attitudes and discouragement brought on by frustration and disillusionment with the attempts to achieve the ideal. The result is a loss of momentum, which is reflected in some recent damaging reports.

There is evidence that deinstitutionalization is not yielding the expected improvements for many retarded persons. Although few studies have compared the treatment models in institutions with programs in group homes, Scheerenberger (1974) has observed: "placements in foster homes, group homes, or nursing homes frequently are more restrictive than residential living in a public facility."

A report to the United States Congress (Comptroller General of the United States, 1977), based on a follow-up study of 164 retarded persons discharged from institutions into the community, reported that "(1) mentally retarded persons were placed in nursing homes where the quality of care was worse than the institution; (2) the treatment administration consisted primarily of medication; and (3) mentally retarded persons were readmitted to institutions because of the lack of community facilities and services."

On the other hand, evidence is mounting on the beneficial effects of community services. For example, Scheerenberger and Felsenthal (1976) found on the basis of interviewing 75 residents and 48 caregivers in community placements in Wisconsin that the residents preferred community living over institutions, formed new friendships within and outside the home, had jobs, and showed progress toward functional independence. O'Connor (1978) described 105 community facilities. Based on interviews of residents and managers, she reported that the facilities typically used one or more types of community services, that developmental plans were available for two-thirds of the residents, and that community opposition had been reduced in one-third of the facilities as a result of the residents' behavior and staff efforts.

Evidence indicates that the quality of community services varies considerably. Writing in *Amicus*, Vitello (1977) has stated:

> The studies ... do not address the many variables which can influence any service model ... what is the age, group and sex of population ... the degree of disability ... funding situation ... effect of the surrounding community? And how well trained are house parents? (p. 43)

As research findings accumulate, they should lead to improved planning based on data that identify successful community alternatives. Vitello (1977) summarizes: "Social policy toward the mentally retarded has reached a critical juncture. . . . It becomes increasingly important that the decision makers use all the information available to them in formulating policy that reflects reason rather than chance."

ATTITUDINAL BARRIERS IN THE COMMUNITY

One obvious conclusion from the evidence is that it is vital to attend to community attitudes when establishing a residential setting. For instance, an Association for Retarded Citizens (ARC) established a townhouse for retarded adults in a large town near Chicago. Initial resistance was mild (8 to 10 neighbors out of a group of 300), and the zoning board approved the project. Now, several years later, the "handful" of original objectors have taken the sponsoring ARC to court for a second time. The neighbors felt they had been "dumped on" once too often. Initially a single-family neighborhood, the zoning was changed to multifamily after a struggle, and a few years later low income housing was developed a block away. When the ARC held an open house prior to the retarded adults moving in, the neighbors descended looking for the "room in the basement where they lock them up when they get violent." Another expected to find all the apartment walls demolished in order to form a dormitory. Still others converged on a large commercial fire extinguisher, required by state fire law, and exclaimed, "Ah-hah! You see it *is* an institution." The open house did little to change attitudes. The hard core objectors took up a collection and returned to court. The majority, who were quite tolerant, left feeling tolerant. The retarded adults moved in and lived there 3 months before any one of the "hard core" knew they were there. There had been no rapes or violence. Property values did not decline, but prejudice dies hard. Stigmatizing terms such as "eternal child," "menace," "mongoloid," "spastic," "violent," and "sexually aggressive" are all familiar expressions, and the misconceptions that they reflect still linger. They may emerge unexpectedly and provoke desperate questions such as one recently asked of Ann Landers: "If I should give birth to a baby that isn't 'right,' can I give it away?"

Goffman (1963), in his book *Stigma*, has written:

> The special situation of the stigmatized is that society tells him he is a member of a wider group which means he is a . . . human being, but that he is also 'different' in some degree, and that it would be foolish to deny this difference. This differentness itself . . . derives from society, for ordinarily before a difference can matter much it must be conceptualized collectively by the society as a whole (p. 100).

But there are signs of change. Advocacy groups such as NARC and the President's Committee on Mental Retardation (PCMR) have been successful in fostering better public education, as well as in influencing legislation and regulations. The increasing recourse to the courts for remedies has been a factor in educating judges and lawyers to the needs of retarded people. For example, Judge Broderick stated in connection with the recent Pennhurst case (*Halderman* v. *Pennhurst State School and Hospital*, (E.D., Pa. 1977), "Since the early 1960s there has been a distinct humanistic renaissance, replete with the acceptance of the theory of normalization for the habilitation of the retarded."

However, as noted by Lippman (1976), public attitudes are still ambivalent:

> NARC's use of communications in the early years made a substantial impact ... but that was an impact of awareness, of replacing a vacuum of ignorance with the substance of information. There is not yet evidence of fundamental changes in public attitudes toward the mentally retarded in the United States in areas of substantive importance such as acceptance of retarded persons as neighbors or as fellow workers (p. 100).

Indeed, the community can be hospitable and cooperative or bare its teeth and erect impenetrable barriers through such means as zoning and cruel discrimination. For example, the Capitol ARC in Lincoln, Nebraska, reported that a survey team telephoned 100 apartment houses with advertised vacancies, stating they were calling for a retarded person who had completed a rehabilitation program and would soon be working and needed a place to live. When landlords learned the identity of the potential tenant, 52 no longer were interested, and 12 felt that a retarded person was not capable of independent living and might not be able to make rent payments. Several others expressed fears about personal safety or property damage. Only one consented to meet the potential tenant.

Kastner, Repucci, and Pezzoli (1978) refer to the documentation by Baker, Seltzer, and Seltzer (1977) of the relationship between public attitudes and the success of community integration of retarded persons. The PCMR contracted with the Gallup Organization (1974) for a survey of community attitudes, which indicated a generally positive acceptance of retarded people by most of society, implying that the process of deinstitutionalization would not be confronted with barriers in the community. The validity of these findings are questionable, however, if consideration is given to the response set that may be generated by "questions which often relate to obvious fundamental human rights and broadly stated equality issues which, given our political and folklore ideologies, leave little realistic room for discriminatory applications in an interview situation" (Kiestner, Wilkins, and Yarrow, 1973).

Kastner, Repucci, and Pezzoli (1978) designed an investigation of community attitudes toward mentally retarded people to reach respondents on a more personal level to extract a more open and honest impression of their actual attitudes. The neighborhoods used in the study were located in a small city of approximately 45,000 and were principally within all white, low to middle income sections. Neighborhoods were classified as in a "threat condition" when houses were for sale and thus were potential sites for group homes. Neighborhoods without houses for sale and at least two or more blocks away from threatening neighborhoods were selected as providing a "control condition." Results revealed the following:

> Although the perceived threat of a group home did not significantly increase negative bias across questionnaire responses, there was evidence that it had impact on respondents when questions affected immediate personal neighborhood interest. ... The fact that more subjects objected to retarded people occupying a group home in their neighborhood when the likelihood was actually presented (threat condition) than when no concrete possibility was mentioned (control condition) indicated that a respondent's expressed attitude may have differed depending upon the circumstances under which the question was asked. ... These studies, in conjunction with current findings, suggest that respondents often evidence a positive attitude toward general issues (e.g., the provision of service programs for retarded people, equal rights, and public education), while indicating disapproval of measures that would actually bring retarded people more closely into their own personal space (e.g., community placement, employment, or a visit from a mentally retarded person, or a retarded person dating a family member). ... The second major finding was the strong relationship between experience with mentally retarded individuals and the more positive attitude toward them ... (Kastner, Repucci, and Pezzoli, 1978, pp. 7-8).

Mamula and Newman (1973) found positive attitudes with neighbors living next to mentally retarded people for at least 2 years. Apparently this prolonged exposure allowed them to discover that retarded people are not harmful or, to be feared. However, exposure may go through several stages, some of which present a few pitfalls for the retarded person. For instance, a social worker in a townhouse for retarded adults recently described to the author the attitude of the neighbors as being patronizing—talking down, buying meals, drinks, and even clothes for the young people. In response to the author's query as to whether the residents perceive this patronizing attitude, the social worker replied: "No, they lap it up and do not consider the consequences." The danger is that retarded people may have difficulty in distinguishing between pity, genuine friendship, and being used.

The study by Kastner, Repucci, and Pezzoli (1978), as well as the experience of many others, concludes that public education for community integration of the retarded is best accomplished by promoting as much public exposure as possible. Exposure is effective through informational modes, such as public campaigns and literature, as well as through increased contact between mentally retarded people and their neighbors. Public education can occur through the cooperation of civic organizations, clubs, neighborhood churches, and schools. Attitudes can be changed if people are approached thoughtfully and sensitively. The use of the media is also valuable, but certain limitations must be recognized. The message must be news or have high public human interest value. Exposes are typically of limited value, because media usually do not follow up to monitor progress and assess change. Rivera (1972), commenting on his expose of Willowbrook, concluded: "The expose has created a climate for change but cannot of itself force change. The burden passes now to the politician who must respond to the will of the people, legislate the reforms and restructure the way we care for our mentally retarded."

SOCIAL BARRIERS

A different type of barrier to integration stems from keeping retarded people in a dependent position. If the retarded person is going to adjust, he must experience, and do; he must be allowed to grow as a person. A Chinese proverb says, "I hear and I forget; I see and I remember; I do and I understand."

An example of how to overcome parents' tendencies to oveprotect their children recently came to the author's attention. One of her retarded friends became overly enthused about apples in a grocery store, purchasing two 8-lb. bags. This left him very little money for other necessities in the diet that week. "If you don't mind," his social worker proposed to his anxious mother, "we'll just let him eat apples this week." Or some parents have been heard to say that there are retarded people who are too handicapped to live in the community. Although it may be true that some individuals will never live independently, they can nonetheless benefit from living in small community-based residences that can provide intimacy, close supervision, and developmental programming. Even though some parents cherish the institution because it symbolizes lifetime permanence and security, the competing advantages of community settings, including a more realistic environment that fosters learning and development, are gradually gaining more supporters.

Resistance to change can be expected whenever the status quo is threatened. Informing parents and gaining their help and support will facilitate change. Likewise, assisting professionals to abandon traditional views of the retarded can help to overcome barriers to change.

Community residences cannot be expected to prosper if the staff who work in them do not receive adequate rewards. Bell (1976) in a study of 39 group homes in Washington, reported that

> Among the principle [sic] causes of stress, of resignations and of termination are problems associated with living in, long hours, emotional strain, confusion about assignments and conflict among staff...we could help them further

their goals, and attract other highly motivated young people by presenting the group home experience as one step in a career ladder...(p. 58).

Considering that many retarded people in group homes are enjoying close relationships with caring adults for the first time in their lives, frequent staff turnovers present a barrier to one of the most unique qualities of a group home.

Any commentary on social/legal and attitudinal barriers would not be complete without at least recognizing the very substantial barriers built up by bureaucrats who avoid decisions, or regulations that contradict or change as soon as the ink is dry. The experience of the Moraine Association illustrates such barriers. The association obtained a bank loan, with some difficulty, to build a community living facility. They used Department of Housing and Urban Development (HUD) Comunity Development (CD) monies of $95,000 as collateral. They raised enough money to build the apartment buildings, and counted on CD block grant money promised for the next year as well, in the sum of $26,000. But the promise was broken. In an effort to reinstate it, the two parents who had initiated the whole project went to the Chicago area HUD office with a lawyer and their county regional planning representative. The regional office claimed that the decision must come from Washington, D.C. The crux of the problem lay with the question raised by the HUD officials regarding eligibility because of the rules' prohibition against residential care on a 24-hour basis (Federal Register, Proposed Rules, Vol. 42, no. 205, 8570, 201 Statute (180, S.C. 5305; P.L. 94-375), 1977). The rules state:

> Centers for the handicapped ... single or multipurpose facility which seeks to assist persons with a physical, mental, developmental ... impairment to become more functional members of the community by providing programs or services which may include, but are not limited to recreation, education, health care, social development independent living ... excluding any facility whose primary function is to provide residential care on a 24-hour a day basis.

The parents then wrote a letter to their congressman, including the following:

> The facility will not provide 24-hour care. It will provide training in independent living skills that cannot be provided any other way. These handicapped young people can learn to shop, cook, keep house and live normally only by doing it ... there are to be no nurses, attendants or other care personnel. Most of the day they will be at work in community jobs ... the young people will be in the facility about six months to one year while they are learning independent living. ...

The wording of the regulations clearly fits the described purpose of the Moraine Association program, yet the bureaucratic runaround given these parents defies reason. The congressmen did answer that they would try to help. One of the parents even made a trip to Washington, D.C. The

$26,000 was eventually released after the grant was rewritten directing the request toward completion of the basement to be used for *recreational* purposes. The community living facility opened in September of 1979 after more than 5 years of effort and struggle. A general rule in dealing with bureaucracies is to know the facts, take the offensive, and remember (and let bureaucrats know) who is the public servant and who is the tax-payer.

LEGAL BARRIERS

Many of the factors described under the rubric of legal barriers have been significant obstacles to the realization of the philosophy of normalization and the principle of the least restrictive environment. Court cases have gradually been chipping away at the automatic decisions of the past to in-stitutionalize retarded people through rulings that support individual habilitation plans and environments that are the least restrictive to the in-dividual's liberty. Furthermore, the court established in *Morales* v. *Turman*, 383 F. Supp. 53 125 (E.D. Texas, 1974), reversed 535 F. 201 864 (5th Circuit 1976), reinstated 430 U.S. 322 (1977), "The fact that the state had not created such a setting or had not established alternative place-ment, could not be a barrier to individual rights." Other cases have gone further and directed the state to affirmatively create community alter-natives.

But, although courts have been contributing to deinstitutionaliza-tion, the legal barrier of zoning has presented a major and sensitive obstacle to the establishment of group homes in stable neighborhoods. As a result, group homes have often been forced to locate in decaying, tran-sient business or in industrial areas.

Zoning statutes are a major land use control that ostensibly are enacted for the health and safety of communities. They specify the types of structures permitted within specific boundaries and the uses to which such structures may be put. For example, industry or places of business may not be established in residential areas.

The most common barrier to group homes is the single-family dwell-ing ordinance that limits residential uses to single families as opposed to multiple families or groups of unrelated individuals. The most restrictive type of ordinance will define "family" as a housekeeping unit related by blood, marriage, or adoption (e.g., *Boraas* v. *Village of Belle Terre*, 476 F. 2nd 806 (2 Cir. 1973)). In *Seaton* v. *Clifford*, 24 Civ. App. 3rd 46, 100 Cal. Rptr. 779 (1972), the court compared a family care home for the mentally retarded to a boarding house and held it to be a business use of property. Administrative bodies sometimes hold that a state licensed home (foster home or group home) is a use requiring medical supervision and, therefore, should be limited to zones with nursing or convalescent hospitals that would therefore be a business use (e.g., *Defoe* v. *San Francisco City Planning Commission*, Civ. No. 30789 San Francisco, Calif. Super. Ct. filed August 17, 1970).

Prejudices that cause people to use these zoning ordinances in a discriminatory fashion center around the myths that the mentally retarded are sexually aggressive, possess a high propensity for criminality, or are just too different to be tolerated. Neighbors also fear disproportionate social costs, decline in property values, overproliferation of group homes for nontraditional living, and loss of community control. This list encompasses some legitimate concerns as well as prejudiced "feelings" unsupported by fact. The denial of granting conditional use permits or zoning variances is often based on these prejudices, and appealing decisions of planning commissions is made more difficult because of the reluctance of courts to review administration decisions without a clear showing of abuse or fraud. Variances are normally granted only to relieve a particular hardship arising from application of a zoning ordinance.

Legal remedies include a preemption by state statute permitting group care facilities, thereby preventing local municipalities from enacting contrary laws and contesting existing zoning ordinances through litigation. States operating under constitutional home rule usually have constitutional provisions limiting the authority of the legislature to intervene in municipal affairs. The California Supreme Court (*Professional Firefighters, Inc.* v. *City of Los Angles*, 60 Cal. 2d 276, 292, 384 P. 2d, 58, 168, 32 Cal. Rptr. 830, 840 (1953)) has ruled that general law prevails over chartered city enactments where the subject matter of the general law is of statewide concern. This is to be determined from the legislative purpose of the law.

When local municipalities pass restrictive zoning ordinances against residential facilities or attempt to enforce what is on the books, constitutional issues may arise regarding due process and equal protection. Thus, the Fourteenth Amendment due process protection can protect the retarded against restrictions that are arbitrary or exclude specific groups. In these cases the facts must be very compelling in challenging the ordinances.

In *Nectow* v. *City of Cambridge,* 277 U.S. 183, 188 (1928), the Supreme Court of Massachusetts stated the principle of zoning:

> The governmental power to interfere by zoning regulations with the general rights of the landowner by restricting the character of his use, is not unlimited; and the other questions aside, such restriction cannot be imposed if it does not bear a substantial relation to the public health, safety, morals or general welfare.

It can be argued that the impact of zoning on group care residential facilities significantly affects the general welfare from the standpoint that viable and potentially productive members of society are prevented from realizing their potential to contribute to society instead of burdening it. Or whenever a community tries to exclude an entire class of individuals because they would be a dangerous nuisance, "...the municipality runs the risk of denying due process by a presumption not universally true...without individual screening" (*Vlandis* v. *Kline*, 412 U.S. 411, 452 (1973)).

In the *Pennhurst* case (*Halderman* v. *Pennhurst*, 1977), Judge Broderick found that "the evidence has been fully marshalled and we find that the confinement and isolation of the retarded in the institution is segregation ... equal protection principles ... prohibit the segregation of the retarded in an isolated institution. ..." Judge Broderick's antisegregation conclusion has far-reaching implications for movement from the institution to the community.

Adjudication can be expensive in time and money, and resistance in many communities makes change laborious. According to a study in January 1978 by the Wisconsin Council on Developmental Disabilities (American Bar Association, 1978), 16 states now have state zoning laws that allow community-based residential services in residential areas (see chapter appendix). The following blueprint for legislative drafters is recommended by Chandler and Ross (1976):

1. A brief declaration of the need for normalizing the lives of developmentally disabled persons
2. A description of how integration in residential zones meets this need
3. A statement emphasizing that uniform integration can occur only through state legislation and that, therefore, the matter is one of statewide concern (the relevant constitutional provisions and preemption cases of the appropriate jurisdiction should be consulted for suggested language
4. A provision making the statute expressly applicable to charter cities (home rule provisions of the state constitution should be consulted)
5. A requirement that the foster home be a permitted use in all residential zones, including, but not limited to, single-family zones
6. A grant of authority to the local entity to impose reasonable condition on use
7. The type of community residential facility referred to in the statute, including the number of residents served and the range of handicaps which they possess, should be based on the licensing classification of small group in the particular jurisdiction (p. 336). [*The Mentally Retarded Citizen and the Law,* edited by Michael Kindred, Julius Cohen, David Penrod, Thomas Shaffer. Copyright © 1976 by The Free Press, a Division of Macmillan Publishing Co.]

Another strategy circumvents the zoning problem entirely and employs the principles and strategies of community organizers. These leaders advocate adopting a positive attitude that avoids the posture that

"You're wrong—we're right," for this causes polarization. The support of the broad community and its leaders must be gained early. The organizer must be aware of people's economic and status needs, and develop tactics that appeal to these needs. Community citizens need to get involved in the project in such a way as to maintain their comfort level, while bringing them into closer physical proximity with retarded people.

CONCLUSION

There is no single answer to knocking down barriers. The situation calls for a careful investigation of law, regulations, and policies. It is essential that a good sound case be developed and documented for the need for community-based residential services. Common sense and tact should be used. Never try to overload a neighborhood with group homes. If a zoning variance or appeal is needed, careful preparation and rehearsal are essential. It is also useful to have sympathizers present.

Finally, establishing a group home or other community-based residential service seems so awesome a task that it is a wonder that projects have indeed succeeded. The barriers are formidable, including social factors, legal obstacles, complex and uncoordinated state fire and safety standards, complex funding streams, and befuddling regulations. Furthermore, poorly run projects endanger the whole community movement and risk giving it a bad name. Despite these obstacles—despite the 5 to 10 years required to create the two projects in the author's county—this writer remains an advocate for the community movement. Her personal experience has led to renewed optimism in that her son, 6 months in a supervised apartment, has matured more in that time than in the previous 5 years. Barriers beware! The unconquered shall be conquered!

REFERENCES

American Bar Association. 1978. Zoning for Community Homes. The Developmental Disabilities State Legislative Project, Washington, D.C. pp. 6–8.

Baker, B., Seltzer, G., and Seltzer, M. 1977. As Close As Possible: Community Residence for Retarded Adults. Little, Brown & Company, Boston.

Bell, C. 1976. Working in Group Homes. Washington State Association of Group Homes, Seattle.

Chandler, J., and Ross, S. 1976. Zoning restrictions and the right to live in the community. In: M. Kindred, J. Cohen, D. Penrod, and T. Shaffer, (eds.), The Mentally Retarded Citizen and the Law, p. 336. The Free Press, New York.

Comptroller General of the United States. 1977. Returning the mentally disabled to the community: Government needs to do more. A report to the United States Congress. U.S. Department of Health, Education, and Welfare, Washington, D.C.

Gallup Organization. 1974. Public attitudes regarding mental retardation. In: R.

Nathan (ed.), Mental Retardation: Century of Decision. U.S. Government Printing Office, Washington, D.C.

Goffman, I. 1963. Stigma. Prentice-Hall, Inc. Englewood Cliffs, N.J.

Kastner, L. S., Repucci, N. D., and Pezzoli, J. 1978. Assessing discrimination versus acceptance of the retarded in the community. Paper presented at the American Psychological Association, August, Toronto.

Kiestner, B., Wilkins, C., and Yarrow, P. 1973. Verbal attitudes and overt behavior involving racial prejudice. In: P. Swingle (ed.), Social Psychology in National Settings. Aldine Publishing Company, Chicago.

Lippman, L. 1976. The public. Changing patterns in residential services for the mentally retarded. Rev. ed. President's Committee on Mental Retardation, Washington, D.C.

Mamula, R. A., and Newman, N. 1973. Community Placement of the Mentally Retarded. Charles C Thomas Publisher, Springfield, Ill. Quoted in L.S. Kastner et al., Assessing discrimination versus acceptance of the retarded in the community, p. 2. Paper presented at the American Psychological Association, August 1978, Toronto.

National Association for Retarded Citizens. 1976. Residential services: Position statements of the National Association for Retarded Citizens. National Association for Retarded Citizens, Arlington, Tex.

National Association for Retarded Citizens and The International League of Societies for the Mentally Handicapped. 1976. A symposium on normalization and integration: Improving the quality of life. Airlie, Va.

O'Connor, G. 1978. Home is a good place. Monogr. No. 2. American Association on Mental Deficiency, Washington, D.C.

Rivera, G. Quoted in A. Shearer, The news media. Changing Patterns in Residential Services for the Mentally Retarded, p. 113. 1972 ed. Vintage Books, Willowbrook, N.Y.

Scheerenberger, R. C. 1974. A model for deinstitutionalization. Ment. Retard. 12 (6):3-7.

Scheerenberger, R. C., and Felsenthal, D. 1976. A study of alternative community placements. Unpublished manuscript.

Vitello, S. J. 1977. Beyond deinstitutionalization: What's happening to the people? Amicus (2), p. 43.

Appendix

STATE STATUTE CHART: State Zoning Laws Regulating

State	Type of Community Facility	Residents	
		No.	Type
ARIZONA Act of June 7, 1978, Ch. 198 §37 (H.B. 2426) (Effective Dec. 1, 1973)	Residential facility	6 or fewer 7 or more	Developmentally disabled persons
CALIFORNIA Welf. & Inst. Code §§5115-5116 (Deering Supp. 1977)	Family care home Foster home Group home	6 or fewer	Mentally disordered or otherwise handicapped persons, or dependent and neglected children
COLORADO Rev. Stat. §§27-10.5-133 (Supp. 1976), 30-28-115 (Supp, 1976)	Group home	8	Developmentally disabled persons
MARYLAND No. 1343, amending Art. 59A, Ann. Code (1972 Replacement Vol. and 1977 Supp.)	Public group home Private group home	4-8	Mentally retarded persons
MICHIGAN Acts of Jan 3, 1977 Pub. L. Nos. 394-396	Residential facility	6 or fewer	Persons in need of supervision or care
MINNESOTA Stat. Ann. §§252.28 (West Supp. 1977), 462.357 (West Supp. 1977)	Group home Foster home Residential facility	6 or fewer 7-16	Mentally retarded or physically handicapped persons

Community Facilities for Developmentally Disabled Persons

Zone in Which Permitted	Con- ditional Use Permits Allowed	State Licensing of Facility		Dispersal of Facilities Required
		Required	Licensor	
Single family Multiple family[1]	No Yes[2]	Yes	Dept. of Eco- nomic Security	1200 ft. required be- tween residential facilities
Single family	Yes	Yes	Not specified	Not specified
Single family	Yes	Yes	Dept. of Health	750 ft. required be- tween facilities
[3] All resi- dential zones	No[4]	Yes Yes[5]	Sec. of Health and Mental Hygiene Director of Men- tal Retarda- tion Admin- istration	Not specified
Single family	Yes	Yes	Director of Dept. of Services	1,500 ft. (3,000 ft. in cities over one mil- lion population) re- quired unless per- mitted by local ordinance
Single family Multiple family	Not specified Yes	Yes	Commissioner of Public Welfare	300 ft. required be- tween facilities un- less conditional use permit is granted

(continued)

STATE STATUTE CHART: State Zoning Laws Regulating

State	Type of Community Facility	Residents No.	Type
MONTANA Rev. Codes Ann. §§112702.1-.2 (Supp. 1977)	Community residential facility: group, foster or other home	8 or fewer	Developmentally disabled or handicapped persons
NEW JERSEY Stat. Ann. §§30:4C-2(m),-26 (West Supp. 1977)	Group home	12 or fewer	Children
NEW MEXICO Act of April 7, 1977, ch. 279 §20 (to be codified in Stat. Ann. §14-20-1)	Community residences	10 or fewer	Mentally ill or developmentally disabled persons
OHIO Act of Aug. 1, 1977, Amended Substitute S.B. No. 71 (to be codified in Rev. Code Ann. §5123.18 [Page])	Family home Group home	8 or fewer 9–16	Developmentally disabled persons
RHODE ISLAND Act of May 13, 1977, ch. 257 (to be codified in Gen. Laws 45-24-22)	Any type of residence	6 or fewer	Retarded children or adults
SOUTH CAROLINA Act of April 4, 1978; H.B. 2121 Amendments to Act 653 of 1976 and 1976 Code §44-21-525, §44-17-10	Community residential facility	9 or fewer	Mentally handicapped persons

Community Facilities for Developmentally Disabled Persons (*continued*)

Zone in Which Permitted	Conditional Use Permits Allowed	State Licensing of Facility		Dispersal of Facilities Required
		Required	Licensor	
Single family	Yes	Yes	Dept. of Health and Environmental Science; Dept. of Social and Rehabilitative Services	Not specified
6	Not specified	7	7	Not specified
Single family	Not specified	Yes	Not Specified	Not specified
Single family Multiple family	Where such ordinance in effect prior to 6/15/77 Yes	Yes	Chief of Division of Mental Retardation and Developmental Disabilities	Not Specified Limitation on excessive concentration of facilities permitted
8	Not specified	No	—	Not specified
Single family[9]	Not specified	Yes	Dept. of Mental Health and Dept. of Mental Retardation	No excessive concentration of community residential facilities

(*continued*)

STATE STATUTE CHART: State Zoning Laws Regulating

State	Type of Community Facility	Residents No.	Type
TENNESSEE 1978 Tenn. Pub. P.C. 863 (H.B. 777)	Community home	8 or fewer	Mentally retarded or physically handi- capped persons
VERMONT Act of March 24, 1978, H. 698 (to be codified in Stat. Ann. tit. 24 §4409(d)	Community care home or group home	6 or fewer	Developmentally disabled or phys- ically handicapped
VIRGINIA Code §15.1-486.2 (Supp. 1977)	Family care home, foster home, group home	Not speci- fied	Mentally retarded and other develop- mentally disabled persons
WISCONSIN Signed into law March 21, 1978; Ch. 205, Laws of 1977	Child welfare agency Group foster home for children Adult residential facility	8 or fewer[11] 9-15 16 or more	All children or adults

Source: American Bar Association. 1978. Zoning for community homes, pp. 6–8. The Developmental Disabilities State Legislative Project, Washington, D.C. Reprinted by permission.

[1] Residential facilities of 7 or more residents are a permitted use in any zone in which residential buildings of similar size, containing rooms provided for compensation, are a permitted use.

[2] Conditional use permits allowed only if no conditions are imposed on such facilities which are more restrictive than those imposed on similar dwellings in the same zone.

[3] The statute is somewhat confusing: "Zoning classifications. Although the public group home is exempt from any local zoning rule or regulation, public group homes may not be located in any area prohibited by the local zoning law. However, for the purposes of the mental retardation law, and zoning, the public group home conclusively shall be deemed a single family residential use, permitted in all residential zones. ..." §19B(b)(5).

[4] Group homes shall not be subject to a special exception or conditional use permit or procedure different from those required for a single family dwelling in the same zone.

[5] Certificate of approval required.

[6] No municipality shall enact an ordinance governing single-family use of land which discriminates between children who are members of single families and children who are placed in group homes.

Community Facilities for Developmentally Disabled Persons (*continued*)

Zone in Which Permitted	Conditional Use Permits Allowed	State Licensing of Facility		Dispersal of Facilities Required
		Required	Licensor	
Single family[10]	Not specified	Not specified	Not specified	Not specified
Single family	Not specified	Yes	Not specified	1,000 ft. required between facilities
Appropriate private residential districts	Yes	Not specified	—	Yes
All residential zones	[12] None Permit required for 1 or 2 family zones Permit required for all residential zones	Yes	Dept. of Health and Social Services	[13] 2,500 ft. distance, and density limit of the greater of 25 or 1% of population in municipality or aldermanic district for class 1–4 cities

[7] Must be recognized as group home by Department of Institutions and Agencies in accordance with state rules and regulations.

[8] Residents are considered a family, and all requirements pertaining to local zoning are waived.

[9] While the South Carolina statute provides that community homes are to be treated as natural families for county or municipal zoning purposes, it also gives the political subdivision the right to object to a proposed location. This objection is made to the State Budget and Control Board, and that Board must make a decision on the objection, if appealed by the state agency, within a given time period. If no decision is made by the Board within the time period, then the political subdivision's objection controls and the location of the community home is prevented.

[10] Group homes of 8 or fewer residents are considered single family residences.

[11] A private, licensed foster home for four or fewer children is permitted, without space or density limits, in all residential areas.

[12] The municipality may annually review the effect of any community facility and may order it to close unless special zoning permission is obtained. The order is subject to judicial review.

[13] The municipality may, at its discretion, agree to increase the density limit or decrease the dispersal distance.

10
BASIC PRINCIPLES AND PHILOSOPHIES FOP DEVELOPING RESIDENTIAL SERVICES IN THE COMMUNITY

Gene Patterson

This chapter reviews some fundamental aspects of a philosophy about residential services as reflected in the Basic Principles adopted by the National Association for Retarded Citizens' (NARC) Position Statements on Residential Services (1976).

Few people have a firm notion about what they should expect from residential services or, for that matter, from any service for mentally retarded individuals. A clearly defined philosophy or theory based on the best scientific and legal understandings available can resolve much of the confusion about the most appropriate service approach for mentally retarded children and adults.

Every workable and useful philosophy is based on a set of principles, or fundamental assumptions about the nature of humanity, the goals of society, and the cultural factors that influence the way individuals think about their status as human beings. These basic principles serve as guides in making decisions about virtually every aspect of life.

Basic principles are different from recipes or rules. Recipes work only if the ingredients are always the same. Sets of complex rules rarely work, since people tend to forget, overlook, or misinterpret them in day-to-day decision making.

People are conditioned by the society in which they live—and by the physical environment in which they develop—to adopt certain basic assumptions that govern how decisions are made (e.g., most children learn early in life that hot surfaces can cause burns, and thus make "automatic" decisions to avoid touching them). Within the realm of social learning, people are also conditioned to think in certain ways about social behaviors and the worthiness of individuals who behave in appropriate or inappropriate ways.

All mental processes for assessing situations and making decisions are based on a collection of assumptions or beliefs that are then organized into working principles. These fundamental principles govern our day-to-day and moment-to-moment behavior. Therefore, making decisions about specific services will be strongly influenced by fundamental assumptions about the nature of mental retardation and about human services in general.

The position statements adopted by the NARC Board of Directors (National Association for Retarded Citizens, 1976) are based upon 13 fundamental principles concerning residential services. These principles are intended to serve as guides and standards in the process of designing, improving, revising, and expanding the provision of services to aid mentally retarded individuals.

CONSTITUTIONAL RIGHTS

Principle 1:   Retarded children and adults are guaranteed the same constitutional rights as other children and adults and may not be deprived of life, liberty, or property, without due process of law; nor shall they be denied equal protection granted by the laws.

The first principle relates directly to devising approaches that will ensure that services are in place in the community and that those services are adequate to meet the needs of retarded individuals. It recognizes that all human service systems must be compatible with the nation's cultural value system and legal guarantees.

The courts have recently clarified many of the legal rights issues associated with services, and it is safe to work from an assumption that the retarded individual enjoys all the same privileges of citizenship as nonhandicapped persons. Only through the legal process can citizenship rights be suspended, and even then the court must conduct periodic reviews to ensure that the individual's rights are restored at the earliest possible time.

It has been noted that the Constitution guarantees the rights to vote, to make contracts, and to enjoy the freedom of thought so closely associated with American government. However, the Constitution does not guarantee that individuals will vote wisely or make good contracts. If, for example, persons were required to make good contracts, the nation's marriage and divorce rates might be considerably different.

RESIDENTIAL FACILITIES

Principle 2:   Residential facilities of all varieties are particularly vulnerable to conditions or situations that can impair the quality of life for the residents whom they serve. Facilities become dehumanizing when they become developmentally counterproductive by violating the dignity of the resident and limiting his or her opportunity to gain "useful knowledge." Dehumanization is a denial of the individual's basic rights to liberty and the pursuit of happiness guaranteed by the United States Constitution.

The second principle recognizes that not all settings or situations are conducive to the optimal development of new skills and successful social behaviors. The idea of something being developmentally counterproductive is a crucially important concept in raising expectations for what a residential service should be. A situation can be considered developmentally counterproductive when it teaches the retarded individual to distrust people, to be dishonest, passive and dull, or socially incompetent.

If a person's life is essentially controlled by power figures who give only minimal information regarding what is being done to and for the person, if the person is led to expect certain events that rarely occur, if he is not trusted and respected or is expected to be incompetent, then that person is being taught to be distrustful, dishonest, and incompetent.

Situations or conditions that interfere with the individual's opportunity to learn are also considered to be developmentally counterproductive. Situations of this type can occur in several areas of human activity. For example, if a person is given no opportunities to practice communicating his ideas, interests, or observations, then he is effectively being taught not to be successul. There are a myriad of techniques to assist even the most severely handicapped person to learn to communicate with other people (e.g., Deich and Hodges, 1977; Michaelis, 1978; Vanderheiden and Harris-Vanderheiden, 1977; Wendt, Sprague, and Marquis, 1975).

If the place where one lives is crowded, uncomfortable, or unsanitary, that environment will interfere with appropriate development, and therefore, becomes developmentally counterproductive to the individual's continued mental and physical growth.

The question of developmentally counterproductive situations and conditions can be examined by a brutally honest assessment of whether a situation encourages new skills or whether it interferes with the learning and practice of personal and social survival skills.

EDUCATIONAL OPPORTUNITIES

Principle 3:   Individuals with retarded mental development have a right to the general social priority of participation in appropriate educational opportunities. Retarded individuals should have those opportunities which will promote their personal development. For example, if they are treated as children throughout their lifetimes, retarded persons are deprived of the opportunity to learn adult behaviors.

This principle is in accord with the NARC's *Policy Statements on the Education of Mentally Retarded Children* (1971), the first of which states:

> Public school education must be provided for all mentally retarded persons, including the severely and profoundly retarded. There should be no dividing line which excludes children from public education services. If current educative technologies and facilities are inappropriate for the education of some retarded persons, then these existing educational regimes should be modified.

The impact of court decisions with respect to the "right to education" upon residential services is discussed by Scheerenberger in Chapter 7.

DEVELOPMENTAL EXPERIENCES

Principle 4:   The purpose of a residential service implies that clients of the service are in need of ongoing developmental experiences which they are unable to receive at home. While the learning needs of both retarded and nonretarded persons are continuous throughout their lifetimes, the retarded individual usually has a more intense need for structured learning situations. By the very nature of their handicap, mentally retarded persons require increased or specialized opportunities to learn new skills. Adults need a continuing program to increase or maintain their skills of independence.

The fourth principle represents a key concept with regard to program expectations. During the past decade, it has become apparent that custodial programs are an inadequate response to the problems of mental retardation. Likewise, federal courts have recognized the inappropriateness of purely custodial approaches, and have mandated active habilitation programs in the "right to treatment" cases brought before them. It is fair then to say that if an individual needs to be admitted to a supervised residential setting, that person also needs an active program designed to teach new skills and to provide those learning opportunities that result in greater independence.

For a range of reasons, many people find the concept of "continuous development" to be oddly discomforting. There is, of course, the understandable tendency to equate "being a student" with one's own experiences in the formal classrooms of our schools and colleges. The student role in these settings is naturally associated with complicated books, homework, and, perhaps worst of all, tests and quizzes. Because of this bias about the uncomfortable role of being a student, there are those who insist that one should not have to be a student after reaching adulthood and, presumably, a state of autonomy.

In reality, however, learning is a continual process, and adults continue to learn new skills, new ideas, and new ways of thinking. Centuries of observations have led to what may be an axiom of humanness—when learning stops, regression and deterioration begin. For those persons with some kind of handicap, the need for continual learning becomes even more apparent.

The residential program should be a secure place in which to learn new skills, and staff members should think of the program's residents as "learners," that is, as students in the process of living. It should be emphasized that continual learning does not necessarily imply a rigid and structured curriculum that occupies every moment of the individual's waking day. There are, however, circumstances in which such a curriculum is probably essential for at least some period of time, depending upon the individual's need. There are programs (e.g., Azrin and Thienes, 1978) that have developed crash-training techniques using behavior modification approaches to teach toileting skills within a one- or two-day time period.

PERSONAL GOALS

Principle 5: Programs for retarded persons must give attention to the individual's personal goals. Most retarded men and women are capable of setting personal goals and communicating their desires and aspirations. Even nonverbal retarded children and profoundly

retarded adults can often participate in decision making and goal setting if given a legitimate opportunity.

The retarded individual and the family or guardian should participate in planning for residential placement and/or program paticipation.

Most parents and professionals will agree that the retarded individual's opinions and interests should be solicited. Often, however, this belief is qualified when thinking about the retarded person's active participation in setting goals and making decisions. There is an understandable tendency to assume that the person is unable to make appropriate decisions because he is mentally retarded. This assumption overlooks the fact that all decisions do not involve major, complex issues, and that people learn to make good decisions through practice. If there are opportunities to decide between alternatives, the individual learns to make better decisions, and thereby becomes somewhat more independent.

As with any interaction with the student, the teacher, or the more knowledgeable person, begins at that point where the student is currently functioning. He uses skills, words, and ideas the student already understands to teach new words, new ideas, and new skills. In the same way, decision-making opportunities must be appropriately simple or difficult, depending upon the capabilities of the student at that moment. For example, if the individual wants a toy, there is an opportunity to practice decision making by offering two toys and forcing a choice between them. At bath time, decisions can be as simple as selecting which ear to wash first.

To survive in this or any society, the individual must become minimally competent in learning to solve problems about day-to-day events and situations. By the very nature of their disability, mentally retarded persons experience slowness and great difficulty in learning and in remembering the associations between those facts and morals that are called into play in solving problems and making decisions. Therefore, to be successful, any program must provide frequent and consistent opportunities to practice problem-solving skills.

Through an expanded electronics technology, there are literally dozens of new devices that permit or facilitate active communication with even the most profoundly handicapped child or adult.

Finally, it should be noted that involvement of the resident and his family in planning program options has value beyond the surface issue of simple fairness. When everyone understands and accepts the specific goals of the program, the chances for success in reaching those goals are dramatically increased.

LIFE-STYLE

Principle 6:   Retarded children and adults should be helped to live as normal a life as possible. The structuring of daily routines, the life-style and the nature of the physical environment should approximate the normal cultural pattern to the greatest extent possible.

The life-style a person leads controls the things he learns and the way he learns to think. The normal life-style is inevitably structured to provide the individual with opportunities to learn and practice those skills that are necessary to maintain that particular life-style. In other words, the personal and social routine of life, the values, attitudes, and skills associated with a particular culture or subculture are learned by growing up and living in that culture.

Several years ago, when the author taught Peace Corps volunteers, there was great concern about a problem called "culture shock." Culture shock occurred when an individual from one culture suddenly was thrust into a strange and different milieu. Often when an individual moves from one culture to another, he experiences rejection by the natives of his new home because he does not yet understand the intricacies and etiquette of this different life-style.

The mentally retarded individual often shares in a similar kind of cultural rejection because he has failed to learn those social skills that make him acceptable as a member of society. It is important, therefore, for the child or adult who has difficulty in learning to have the benefit of regular, consistent, and practical experiences in developing social skills. The best way to learn to live in a community is to actually live there.

A residential program must provide the experience of a normal life-style as an essential part of the service. Also, the resident must have consistent opportunities to practice necessary skills in normal situations.

THE DEVELOPMENTAL MODEL

Principle 7:   Retarded children and adults are capable of learning and development. Each individual has potential for progress, no matter how severely handicapped he or she might be.

Principle 8:   The basic goal of programming for retarded persons consists of maximizing the individual's personal, social, and vocational development, and as such is identical with the goal of educating and socializing all other citizens. The adequacy of programs, as well as of physical and psychological environments, can be evaluated in terms of the degree to which they fulfill this goal.

In general, this goal is more rapidly met by including the retarded individual within the mainstream of society or by replicating
the patterns and physical characteristics of the prevailing culture
when it is necessary for a retarded person to live away from his or her
natural home.

Principle 9: Specific program objectives must be tailored to meet
the needs of each individual, and will vary for different degrees of impairment. The most feasible and constructive approach, in view of
current limitations of knowledge, is to assume that most retarded
persons have the potential for greater mental, physical, and social
development and for eventually leading an independent life-style.
This approach must dominate program planning until the
individual's response to appropriate programs clearly reveals his or
her inability to attain this goal.

Principle 10: All programs for retarded persons must meet the
three basic criteria of the developmental model:

1. Contribute to increasing the complexity of the individual's
   behavior
2. Contribute to increasing the individual's ability to control his or
   her environment
3. Contribute to maximizing those qualities that have been designated as "normal" or human

The seventh, eighth, ninth, and tenth principles all relate to a recognition and endorsement of the developmental model. Wolfensberger
(1972) and others have advocated a developmental model as the most
desirable concept of mental retardation. The developmental model takes
an optimistic view of the modifiability of behavior, and usually it does not
invest the differences of the retarded person with strong negative value.
Even severely retarded individuals are perceived as capable of growth,
development, and learning.

Over the past several years, a wide range of research studies has con-
tributed a mass of compelling evidence to support the belief that retarded
individuals are, indeed, capable of learning and development, and that
each retarded person has potential for progress no matter how severely
handicapped he may be. There is no justification, with the possible exception of rare cases of unremitting coma, for assigning any child or adult to
a hopeless category.

There are still programs in this country that label certain individuals
as having reached their potential for development, and thus assign them
to custodial or maintenance programs. Such expectations are perhaps in
conflict with both scientific knowledge and citizenship guarantees.

At an earlier time, one of the most often noted and socially sanctioned goals for the institutionalized individual was his rapid adjustment
to institutional life. Subgoals included obedience to rules and regulations,
acceptance of institutional routines, compliance with the moral code of
the attendants, and relinquishment of strong emotional ties to the family.
Such goals are now recognized as inappropriate and intolerable.

Individuals in any residential program should be constantly challenged to learn new skills and to exert greater control over their own
behaviors. Whatever skill the individual has can always be used to learn
another, slightly more complex task, requiring slightly more controlled
mental activity. The same logic applies when considering all developmental tasks, including social and vocational skills.

Assessment and evaluation of a particular residential service are
necessarily based on whether or not the clients of that service continue to
make gains in their individual growth and development. To meet this
rigorous, evaluative criterion, service providers must operate their programs in such a way as to employ all available knowledge about factors
that influence human development. Those factors include the quality of
human interactions within an environment and whether those interactions
are conducive to learning new skills.

The ninth principle is drawn from the knowledge that what actually
happens in a situation most often reflects the expectations held by the
people involved. That is, people generally achieve no more than what
they expect, or are expected, to achieve.

The rich but stormy history of mental retardation services clearly
reveals the truth of this principle. The extremely limited expectations
commonly held about the potential of retarded persons were demonstrated
in a repetition of program failures within institutions throughout the
world. Programs were not designed to capitalize on whatever skills the
individual might have because it was assumed that he either could not or
did not need to learn.

However, as professionals and parents came to realize the detrimental impact of their low expectations, a flurry of fresh research began
to reveal more positive information about the disability called "mental
retardation." One of the many benefits derived from this increased
understanding is the concept of an individually designed program plan.

The program plan must be based on a careful assessment of the
individual's current skills and current limitations. In other words, the
plan should be like a map—showing the individual's current level of
development, giving a clear idea of where he is going, and providing a
sequence of moves to get there. The program plan is a statement of expectations for individual development and is, of course, subject to modification and expansion as the individual progresses.

Given the importance of an individualized program plan (IPP), the question arises as to how to determine whether it is a good plan.

Knowing where one wants to be is often easier than knowing how to get there. There are, however, some criteria, or "guide posts," to help in constructing and evaluating a program plan. These criteria provide general directions and things to look for along the way.

The overriding goal of all programs is to help the individual to survive in the most normalized environment possible for that person. Survival is thus defined as effective coping with the environment, rather than simply the preservation of life.

An important aspect of fostering coping behavior is the selection of program goals that will lead to increasingly complex behaviors. The desirability of fostering complex patterns of behavior is illustrated by the fact that such behaviors are more frequently demanded by a technological and increasingly sophisticated society. Hence, they enable the retarded person to begin taking advantage of the more complex opportunities available in American society instead of remaining totally dependent on others throughout his life cycle.

A second criterion for use in determining program goals is the extent to which they increase the individual's ability to control his environment and to make choices among alternatives, rather than being passively controlled by the events and things around him. Retarded persons should thus be helped to develop behaviors that will extend their control over the environment, including other persons and themselves.

The third, and in some ways the most basic criterion for determining programmatic goals is the concept of maximizing the human qualities of each individual. In this context, "human qualities" refer to those behavioral characteristics culturally designated as "normal" or "human." Obviously, these characteristics differ from culture to culture and from era to era within the same culture.

Our culture defines relatively flexible parameters for behaviors considered acceptable during most stages of development, such as infancy, adolescence, and adulthood. The individual whose behavior consistently violates cultural expectations may be labeled as "deviant," and is in danger of social isolation. For retarded persons, then, this principle implies attempting to develop basic social behaviors that are appropriate to the individual's stage in the life cycle.

Human qualities include such attributes as the ability to determine one's own goals and the strategies to accomplish them—spontaneity, enthusiasm, initiative in interpersonal relationships, and myriad other behavioral characteristics judged desirable by contemporary society.

In a fascinating study of the community adjustment of deinstitutionalized mentally retarded persons, Gollay et al. (1978) discovered several important relationships between successful community adjustment and existing community services. Those individuals who had the opportunity to participate in more community programs and who received more of their needed services from local community agencies made better adjustments and were less likely to return to the institutional settings. In general, those who successfully adapted to community living appear to have been more actively involved in utilization of community support services and training, and in participation in day placement activities, leisure time activities, and friendships.

UTILIZATION OF COMMUNITY SERVICES

Principle 11:   Programs for mentally retarded persons should utilize the community's existing services to the fullest extent. Utilization of community services provides opportunities for the retarded person to experience a broader array of social situations which can contribute to learning new skills and increasing independence.

Utilization of general community services also provides opportunities to sensitize community agencies to the service needs of retarded individuals and their families.

Evidence from the few formal studies available underscores the validity of this principle. For example, in the report of their study of adjustment to the community following deinstitutionalization, Gollay et al. (1978) concluded that "... mentally retarded persons living in communities which have a wide range of services, training and residential options available to them do better than those mentally retarded people living in communities with fewer services. The more support available to the community the more likely is the mentally retarded person to remain in the community, to be more active, to have fewer problems, to have more independence, and to have fewer unmet needs."

A COMPREHENSIVE SYSTEM OF SERVICES

Principle 12:   A comprehensive system of community services must be developed to provide for:

1. **Early identification of handicaps that are developmentally disabling**
2. **Early assistance to correct or alleviate those disabilities and a continuity of services to thereby reduce the need for residential services**

3. Ongoing services to the individual and family to ensure the greatest possible gains in development

There is a fairly widespread and understandable confusion about the meaning of a "comprehensive" system of services. Webster's dictionary defines *comprehensive* as "inclusive" and "covering completely." A comprehensive community service system would, therefore, be one that was able to respond to any service need presented by a citizen of the community.

Three types of services are particularly applicable to mentally retarded individuals and their families. It is especially important to identify every child who has some handicap that could cause mental retardation. Identification of these children should occur as soon after birth as is technically possible. When a handicapped or disabled child is located, a service system should respond without delay to correct the disability or to reduce its impact on the child's growth and learning. Evidence from successful infant development programs indicates that many of the disabling consequences of disease, birth defects, and brain injury can be significantly reduced. Thus, the earlier a handicapped child is identified and provided with needed services, the less likely he is to require extensive and complex services later in life.

Finally, when helpful, ongoing services are available to the individual *and* his family, there are fewer complications in the continued development of that family. When family members are helped to understand and successfully cope with a child's handicap, there is less likelihood of a need for early placement of that child in some type of residential program. Such early and continued services also reduce the incidence of family disruption, and thereby contribute to a more constructive home environment for the personal development of all family members.

SOCIAL INTEGRATION

Principle 13: Community services should be strategically located throughout the state, region, or county to promote maximum social integration of disabled citizens into the community.

Observations by most social and behavioral scientists support the idea that mentally retarded and other disabled individuals should not be congregated in large groups, but should be integrated within the mainstream of a community's life. Small groups have greater social and learning opportunities. To achieve the goal of integration, it is necessary that services and facilities be dispersed throughout the community. It should be stressed, however, that dipersal does not imply isolation or lack of coordination.

CONCLUSION

These are the basic principles that, in light of current knowledge, the NARC has said must govern the provision of residential services.

Each principle can be reflected in a variety of specific service activities. They are positive principles rather than a sequence of prohibitions. It is up to service providers and advocates to monitor and assess the extent to which these principles are reflected in a specific program.

It has been said that a real patriot is the individual who, when he receives a parking ticket, rejoices that the system works. Perhaps there is an analogy here for those persons who have been, are being, or will be brought before the courts of justice to clarify the way services are provided. The system may be working.

REFERENCES

Azrin, N. H., and Thienes, P. M. 1978. Rapid elimination of enuresis by intensive learning without a conditioning apparatus. Behav. Ther. 9:342–354.

Deich, R. G., and Hodges, P. M. 1977. Language without Speech. Brunner/Mazel, Inc., New York.

Foxx, R. M., and Azrin, N. H. 1973. Toilet Training the Retarded. Research Press, Champaign, Ill.

Gollay, E., Freedman, R., Wyngaarden, M. and Kurtz, M. 1978. Coming Back: The Community Experiences of Deinstitutionalized Mentally Retarded People. Abt Books, Cambridge, Mass.

Michaelis, C. T. 1978. Communication with the severely and profoundly handicapped: A psycholinguistic approach. Ment. Retard. 16:346–349.

National Association for Retarded Citizens. 1971. Policy Statements on the Education of Mentally Retarded Children. National Association for Retarded Citizens, Arlington, Tex.

National Association for Retarded Citizens. 1976. Position Statements on Residential Services. National Association for Retarded Citizens, Arlington, Tex.

Vanderheiden, G. C., and Harris-Vanderheiden, D. 1977. Developing effective modes for response and expression in nonvocal, severely handicapped children. In: P. Mittler (ed.), Research to Practice in Mental Retardation: Education and Training, Vol. II. University Park Press, Baltimore.

Wendt, E., Sprague, M. J., and Marquis, J. 1975. Communication without speech. Teach. Except. Child. 8:38–39.

Wolfensberger, W. 1972. The Principle of Normalization in Human Services. National Institute on Mental Retardation, Toronto.

11

THE RIGHT TO LIVE IN THE COMMUNITY
The Legal Foundation

Frank Laski

The National Association for Retarded Citizens (NARC) and its state units all have long-standing, well-established, and clearly articulated policies and objectives to promote community living and community services for retarded persons. A growing number of state associations are vigorously pursuing those policies and objectives through litigation carefully designed to replace institutions with services in the community. Pennsylvania, first, in *Halderman* v. *Pennhurst State School and Hospital*, 446 F. Supp. 1295 (E.D. Pa. 1977), and Michigan, second, in *Michigan Association for Retarded Citizens* v. *Smith* (1978), have now been joined in the federal courts by Connecticut, Rhode Island, Colorado, Washington, Kentucky, and Florida. The targets include the traditional nineteenth century institutional model, such as Pennhurst State School and Hospital, the newer 1950s versions such as Plymouth Center, and those not yet constructed (*Kentucky Association for Retarded Citizens* v.

This chapter is adapted from the Brief of the Pennsylvania Association for Retarded Citizens, et al., submitted to the U.S. Third Circuit Court of Appeals in *Halderman* v. *Pennhurst*, 446 F. Supp. 1295 (E.D. Pa. 1977). The Brief was prepared by Thomas K. Gilhool, Edward A. Stutman, and Frank Laski, all of the Public Interest Law Center of Philadelphia. The work of the Law Center on Pennhurst and other litigation on behalf of developmentally disabled people is supported financially by the Developmental Disabilities Advocacy Network of Pennsylvania, Inc., and the Developmental Disabilities Office, U.S. Department of Health, Education, and Welfare.

Department for Human Resources and Excepticon, Inc., 1978). Also implicated is the new generation of nursing homes, annexes, and satellite institutions that are fed and nourished by the deinstitutionalization movement. All of this litigation is premised on the right of retarded people to live in the community and has the single purpose of creating community services of sufficient quantity and quality to replace the institutions. This chapter addresses the legal principles that provide the foundation for securing the right to live in the community.

THE RIGHT TO LIVE IN THE COMMUNITY

The right to live in the community is simply defined and its elements are evident in the themes and teaching of this volume. The right to participate in the community and the right to services in the community to make that participation possible are the two basic elements of the retarded person's rights to live in the community. Two examples from the *Pennhurst* trial (*Halderman* v. *Pennhurst*, 1977) serve to illustrate the meaning of the right to live in the community: 1) the testimony of Herman Vaughn, a former resident of Pennhurst, and 2) the testimony of Madge Bolin, a residential program supervisor in Philadelphia.

During the *Pennhurst* trial, the author had the responsibility and privilege to present, as a witness, Herman Vaughn, a man approximately 30 years old who had formerly been a resident of Pennhurst and who was classified by that institution as severely retarded. At the end of his direct examination, Mr. Vaughn was asked to explain to the court the difference between living at Pennhurst and living in Chester County. He testified, "You have more freedom in Chester. In Pennhurst you have no downtown at all. In Pennhurst you cannot do anything you want. ..." Mr. Vaughn lived with foster parents in Chester, worked in a department store in a suburban shopping mall, served as an usher in his foster father's church, and collected stereo records. As far as he was concerned, the right to live in the community was simply the right to be there, that is, the right to participate. However, for many retarded people who are in the community now and who will continue to be there, a second component is necessary, as illustrated by the testimony of another Pennhurst witness, Madge Bolin.

Ms. Bolin, Residential Program Supervisor of a group home for six young men, ages 9 to 17, in Northwest Philadelphia where she and her husband live, testified about two people who previously lived at Pennhurst. Both had severe behavior problems when they came from Pennhurst: one ate newspapers, had daily tantrums, bit and hit other children, broke furniture, and defecated regularly in his pants and in bed. Several notes from school stated that his behavior was uncontrollable and intolerable. The second resident was obstreperous at home, had frequent tantrums, used loud obscenities and frequently messed his pants. Shortly after their placement in the community, they stopped defecating in their pants or in bed. Reports from school show the first young man to be a model student who is extremely cooperative. He interacts very well with other residents and with the neighbors, even though he is still nonverbal. The second young man has grown in social skills and in the ability to communicate with other people and he no longer has tantrums.

As Ms. Bolin testified about the process of adjustment for these two young men and their integration into the life of the community, the judge interrupted and asked, "Is it your testimony, therefore, that they learned to adapt to their surroundings... how long did that take?"

Ms. Bolin replied: "With one of the guys it took about six months; and with the other guy it took about a month."

The young men living in Northwest Philadelphia with Ms. Bolin and her husband attend the public schools, use the neighborhood recreation fields and parks, visit the local dentist, local hospital, and local speech therapist, and regularly use other services in the community. In short, not only are they in the community, but they are part of it. They are living in a community and have effective access to services so that they can grow and develop.

The testimony of Herman Vaughn and Madge Bolin not only clearly defines the right to live in the community but establishes a good part of the factual predicate for the legal basis for this fundamental right. The facts upon which the constitutional equal protection holding and the federal statutory Section 504 (of the Rehabilitation Act of 1973) holding rest are:

1. No one need be confined in an institution;[1] the segregation of retarded people in such places is unnecessary to their effective care and treatment.
2. Services provided in that segregated institutional setting are not, have never been, and cannot be effective services.
3. Each retarded person now institutionalized, and each at risk of segregation in an institution is competent to learn, grow, and live, but can only do so when services are provided in small-scale, integrated community settings.

---

[1] As used here and in the specific cases discussed, the term *institution* is used in Goffman's (1961) sense as "a place of residence and work where a large number of like situated individuals, cut off from the wider society for an appreciable period of time, together lead an enclosed formally administered round of life."

These facts have now been put before the courts in many ways, but perhaps have been presented most vividly and most persuasively by contrasting the lives of retarded persons in the community and the lives of their disabled counterparts or "twins" still in the institution. In the *Pennhurst* case, for example, the "twins" of the young men described in Ms. Bolin's testimony were in Ward C-13 at Pennhurst. The contrast was stark. Expert witness Linda Glenn testified that the men in the community enjoyed " ... a big beautiful and very comfortable, home-like environment ..." where " ... they are involved in a real live house, not an artificial type of environment. . . ." Their counterparts on Ward C-13 are denied even the rudiments of a homelike setting; when they shower or use the toilet they have no privacy at all but are in full view of employees and other residents. In Ward C-13, as in others, life is noisy, rushed, and chaotic.

The differences in skills, in competences realized, and in the quality of life between similarly retarded and otherwise disabled people, marked only by whether they live in an institution or in small-scale, integrating, and individualizing community settings, were systematically displayed on the trial record in the *Pennhurst* case. For each disability grouping on the wards of Pennhurst, whatever the severity of their disability configuration, there are similarly disabled people living in the community-based residential arrangements and receiving services in the community. Whatever the severity of the disability configuration—mildly retarded, moderately retarded, severely or profoundly retarded, or multiply handicapped—the lives of those in normalized environments are starkly different. Their lives are richer in experience and in possibility, fuller in competencies realized, and enjoyed—in short, they are decent lives, as close as possible to the lives of normal people.

THE RIGHT TO EQUAL CITIZENSHIP

The brief submitted to the Third Circuit Court of Appeals in the *Pennhurst* case by the National Association for Retarded Citizens, Epilepsy Foundation of America, and United Cerebral Palsy Associations sets out in detail, ward by ward, community program by community program, the matched sets of "twins," demonstrating that each person at Pennhurst has a "twin" in the community. Those facts form the practical basis for translating the right to live in the community into the legal principle of the right to equal citizenship. Professor Karst (1977) has written:

> The principle of equal citizenship presumptively insists that the organized society treat each individual as a person, one who is worthy of respect, one who belongs. Stated negatively, the principle presumptively forbids the

organized society to treat an individual either as a member of an inferior or dependent caste or as a non-participant.

That principle of equal citizenship had its application by the district court in the *Pennhurst* case and had its first articulation some years ago by Professor Robert Burt of Yale in the President's Committee's landmark volume, *Mentally Retarded Citizens and the Law,* in an article entitled "Beyond the Right to Rehabilitation" (1976). Professor Burt highlighted the need to move from a constitutional notion of a due process of right to treatment or right to habilitation to a right to equal citizenship, a right to live in the community. He stated:

Proposing a right to habilitation for institutionalized residents raises difficulty. If the state owes even minimal habilitation obligations (i.e., medical care, food, clothing) to institutionalized citizens, why does it not owe the same obligations to all citizens? Distinction may be drawn to avoid this and other difficulties, but a more satisfactory alternative rationale for *Wyatt* is readily available. Subtle distinctions need not be drawn if the *Wyatt* right is conceptualized as a right to equal state services for all citizens. As in *PARC* (the right to education case), the court is not requiring the state to provide educational facilities for children in general. But if the state chooses to provide services for some, it must provide some such services to all.

Starting from the proposition that a right to service is not grounded in any substantive right to any particular service, including education, but that if the state chooses to provide that service to any of its citizens, the right to equal services applies to all, including mentally retarded citizens, Burt continues:

The *PARC* theory can and should mean that any state program that segregates mentally retarded citizens as such from others is highly suspect and that courts will require states to treat mentally retarded persons indistinguishably from others, except in ways that are both very limited and very clearly beneficial to the individual. By this test, segregation of the mentally retarded in a remote large-scale institution could never pass constitutional muster. . . .

Burt's analysis of moving from a due process right to treatment to equality of services is firmly based on the U.S. Supreme Court opinion of *Brown* v. *Board of Education*, 347 U.S. 483 (1954). Here the Supreme Court struck down categorically another nineteenth century institution, the segregation of people by race. In *Brown,* after finding that "to separate (children) . . . solely because of their race . . . may affect their hearts and minds in ways unlikely ever to be undone" and has a "detrimental effect," the court announced: "Therefore, we hold that the plaintiffs and others similarly situated for whom the actions have been brought are, by reason of segregation complained of, deprived of the equal protection of the laws guaranteed by the Fourteenth Amendment" (347 U.S. at 495).

With motives identical to the motives leading to racial segregation, the state's intention in creating Pennhurst was to segregate people. The same era that invented Jim Crow laws to segregate people by race created the institution. The Pennsylvania General Assembly declared the purpose of the institution as follows: "Be it enacted, that the Eastern Pennsylvania State Institution for the Feeble-Minded and Epileptic shall be devoted to the segregation ... of epileptic, idiotic, imbecile, or feeble-minded persons" (Act of June 12, 1913 §1, 32 Laws of Pennsylvania 494).

The segregation of retarded people and their classification for purposes of segregation and receipt of services offend and violate the equal protection clause of the Fourteenth Amendment.

The institution demarks two unconstitutional classifications: one between retarded people and all other people who use public services every day without having to submit to segregation, and a second between retarded people themselves. The first classification differentiates those who are required to submit to segregation as the condition of using services from the generality of citizens who may avail themselves of governmental services of a wide and encompassing variety (foster care, family welfare services, counseling, recreation, employment services, zoning, street cleaning, transportation, protection, adult education, and public health services) without segregation and without surrendering freedom or a normal life. For no other group in society, except prisoners, is incarceration permitted, let alone required, as a condition of extending services at all, so that if one chooses services one surrenders freedom and if one chooses freedom one surrenders services.

The second classification demarked by the institution differentiates two classes of retarded people, indistinguishable from one another with respect to their need for effective, individualizing services. Each class has the capacity to benefit from such services, but one class, most of them *not* moderately, severely or profoundly retarded, or multiply disabled, is composed of people who receive effective individualizing services and the other, most of them profoundly, severely or moderately retarded, or multiply disabled, are segregated and not effectively served at all.

Both classifications implicate fundamental rights and, for retarded people in the disfavored class, destroy them. As the price of "services" and "care," the state exacts the surrender of these constitutional rights, thus conditioning unconstitutionally—as it does for almost no other group in our society—the use of public services. To receive the sustenance of the institution, the plaintiff class must give up liberty, the freedoms of association, the freedoms of expression, and the right to family integrity.

While it is clear that the classifications to which retarded people have been subjected are inherently suspect, there is no need to make that showing. The classifications are without rational basis.

The equal protection clause of the Fourteenth Amendment requires that a classification bear some rational relationship to a legitimate state purpose.

What is the purpose of the institution? The state of Pennsylvania in its brief to the Court of Appeals stated: "The rationality of Pennhurst is plainly obvious; there are presently no suitable alternatives." That was their rationale. However, the order of the district court was an order for them to create those alternatives.

If the state's purpose is to protect retarded people, the facts are that the institution does not protect them, but destroys them. If the state's purpose is to teach retarded people so that they can return to the community, the facts at Pennhurst showed that such learning is impossible, that the institution defeats learning, and that few people ever returned from Pennhurst to the community in the 70 years of its existence.

In fact, the purpose of Pennhurst, in reality, is the purpose that the legislature set forth; it is to segregate retarded people for its own demeaning sake, to set aside people who are different and hold them aside. Yet it has been clear since *Brown* that segregation is constitutionally impermissible.

STATUTORY BASIS FOR THE
RIGHT TO LIVE IN THE COMMUNITY

An equal protection doctrine is sufficient in itself to provide a firm foundation for the right to live in the community. However, there is now a federal statutory basis for securing effective community services in the most integrated community setting. The statute is Section 504 of the Rehabilitation Act of 1973 (P.L. 93–112). It will be the most frequently relied upon basis by which the courts will secure the rights of retarded and other disabled people.

In 1973, acting in the exercise of its powers under §5 of the Fourteenth Amendment to enforce Equal Protection of the Laws, Congress enacted Section 504, popularly known as the Civil Rights Act for disabled people. Congress used the exact words from Title VI of the Civil

Rights Act of 1964, and extended its integration imperative to include all handicapped individuals. Section 504 of the Rehabilitation Act of 1973 provides:

> No otherwise qualified handicapped individual in the United States, shall, solely by reason of his handicap, be excluded from participation in, be denied the benefits of, or be subjected to discrimination under any program or activity receiving Federal financial assistance.

The predicate of Congressional enactment of Section 504 was Congress's recognition of the competence of disabled people, of the conditions necessary to the realization of their competences, and of their right to participation as equal citizens. Congress acknowledged the principles of normalization and acted upon them.

Segregation of disabled people was the evil Congress legislated to overcome. Eliminating segregation, Congress found, required an end to the isolation of disabled people and the provision of effective services.

In the *Pennhurst* case the district court held " ... that Section 504 ... imposes affirmative obligations on state and local governmental officials and that under Section 504 unnecessarily separate and minimally inadequate services are discriminatory and unlawful." The court found Pennhurst to be unnecessarily separate for every one of its current residents and all members of plaintiff class; it found the services provided at Pennhurst *not* to be minimally adequate and the services provided in the community insufficient to avoid placement at Pennhurst.

The language of Section 504, its history, the history of related enactments, its administrative construction, and judicial decisions enforcing it make clear that in enacting Section 504 Congress:

1. Required that the segregation of disabled people be ended
2. Prohibited unnecessarily separate services and required that services be provided in the most integrated settings
3. Required that disabled people be admitted equally to all services and to the equal benefit of all services
4. Required that disabled people be provided services equally effective as those provided to other disabled people and as those provided to the general population

The legislative history of Section 504 clearly shows that integrated community alternatives to institutions and services to secure the right to live in the community were central to the Congressional purpose.

Congress considered Section 504 and advanced it to enactment over a period of 2 years. Introduced in the House on December 9, 1971, and in the Senate on January 20, 1972, and framed initially as an amendment to the Civil Rights Act of 1964, Section 504 was eventually co-sponsored by 60 members of the House and 20 Senators. It was ultimately enacted as a part of the Rehabilitation Act of 1973, over two presidential vetoes, by a nearly unanimous Congress.

The problems that Section 504 was intended to overcome were stated clearly by the late Senator Hubert Humphrey, its primary sponsor in the Senate:

> The fundamental fact that one confronts is ... the segregation of millions of Americans from society—suggesting a disturbing viewpoint that these people are not only forgotten but ... expendable.
>
> This bill responded to an awakening public interest in millions of handicapped children, youth, and adults who suffer the profound indignity and despair of isolation, discrimination and maltreatment (118 Congressional Record S9495, March 22, 1972).

Congressman Vanik, introducing Section 504 in the House, said:

> The masses of the handicapped live and struggle among us, often shunted aside, hidden and ignored. How have we as a nation treated these fellow citizens?
>
> In this country we still have the snakepit mental institutions—institutions for confinement without treatment, where brutality and unexplained deaths are common. ... Our governments tax these people, their parents and relatives, but fail to provide services for them. ... The opportunities provided by the Government almost always exclude the handicapped. ...
>
> Today the handicapped are generally a hidden population. ... But the time has come when we can no longer tolerate the invisibility of the handicapped in America (117 Congressional Record H4974-75, December 9, 1971).

Thus, from its origination, the bill especially addressed retarded people in institutions. Introducing Section 504 in the Senate, Senator Humphrey (1972) said:

> I am calling for public attention to three-fourths of the Nation's institutionalized retarded people who live in public and private residential facilities which are more than 50 years old, functionally inadequate and designed simply to isolate these persons from society. ...
>
> These people have the right to live, to work to the best of their ability—to know dignity to which every human being is entitled. But too often we keep children, whom we regard as "different" or a "disturbing influence" out of our schools and community activities altogether. ... Where is the cost-effectiveness in ... consigning them to "terminal" care in an institution?
>
> These are people who can and must be helped to help themselves (118 Congressional Record S525, January 20, 1972).

The Congressional intention that Section 504 be the keystone to the statutory right to live in the community is confirmed by a review of the related enactments of Congress in the 7 years Section 504 was pending, enacted, and amended.

The 91st, 92nd, and 93rd Congresses enacted several statutes that, with Section 504, constitute a new charter for disabled people. Throughout these enactments, Congress acted to purge historic stereotypes of disabled people and the prejudice that arises from them. Furthermore, Congress also mandated that historic patterns of segregation be reversed, that services be extended to severely disabled people, and that severely disabled people be included in the national life. In short, Congress enacted an integration imperative.

In the Rehabilitation Act of 1973, the Congress worked a profound change in the law governing vocational rehabilitation, and required that priority in vocational rehabilitation services be given to "those with the most severe handicaps." For decades, vocational rehabilitation services had been directed to the mildly disabled, reflecting the judgment that severely disabled people were incapable of gainful employment and could not benefit from vocational rehabilitation services. The congressional finding of fact was not only that severely disabled people can learn, but that, given proper services, they can learn productive vocational skills and "engage in gainful employment." The same Congress, in Section 503 of Title V of the Rehabilitation Act of 1973, required government contractors to take affirmative action to employ disabled people, including severely disabled people.

The Education Acts of 1974 and 1975, 20 U.S. Code §1401 et seq., are premised in the same Congressional finding about the competence of severely retarded people. Both Education Acts adopt the principles of normalization, recognize individualization as a necessary condition of learning, growth, and development by retarded people, and place a priority on service to children with the most severe handicaps. Both acts state their own integration requirement, based upon the same findings and with similar purposes as Section 504's integration imperative: That, to the maximum extent appropriate, handicapped children, including children who are in public or private institutions, shall be educated with children who are not handicapped. Even Title XIX (State Medicaid) of the Social Security Act of 1971 which, through administrative subversion at the federal level and short-sighted greed at the state level, has been converted to pay for nonservice in institutions, demonstrates clearly the Congressional intention to move away from institutions and into the community.

The same Congress that, in 1971, included "health or rehabilitative services for mentally retarded ... in a public institution" within the definition of "intermediate care facility services" fundable under Title XIX of the Social Security Act, affirmatively required, as a condition of funding, "independent professional review ... of each patient's need for intermediate care ... *prior to admission* ... in an intermediate care facility ... with respect to ... the necessity and desirability of the continued placement of such patients in such facilities and the feasibility of meeting their health care needs through alternative institutional or noninstitutional services."

One purpose of these amendments, responding to "the failure of many states" to provide appropriate placements, was "to assure ... that each person is in the right place at the right time receiving the right care" (117 *Congressional Record* 44721, 1971). The second purpose was to contribute funding to help underwrite "the active provision of rehabilitative, educational and training services to enhance the capacity of mentally retarded individuals to care for themselves or to engage in employment."

In 1976, cognizant that the procedures put in place by the 1971 amendments to encourage deinstitutionalization and the creation of alternative facilities were having only limited effect and that further incentives for the creation of alternatives to institutions such as Pennhurst were necessary, Congress, in the Social Security Amendments of 1976, changed significantly the "set-off" provisions of Titles XVI (Supplemental Security Income) and XIX (State Medicaid) of the Social Security Act of 1971. Previously, no one in a Title XIX funded "public institution" was eligible for a Supplemental Security Income (SSI) grant under Title XVI. As incentive to the creation of small community-based residential facilities, Congress amended Title XVI to except "community residences which serve no more than 16 residents" from the definition of "public institution" and hence to eliminate for them, uniquely among public institutions, the SSI "set-off."

These related enactments and their intertwining legislative histories confirm that Congress intended Section 504 to charter a new status for disabled people and to affirmatively require that disabled people, especially those severely disabled and retarded, be included in every aspect of national life. The common purpose of these acts was best articulated by Congress itself in the White House Conference on Handicapped Individuals Act (1974):

> The Congress finds that ... it is essential that recommendations be made to assure that all individuals with handicaps are able to live their lives independently and with dignity, and that the complete integration of all individuals with handicaps into normal community living, working and service patterns be held as the final objective (Sec. 301(6), 29 U.S.C.A. Sec. 701N, December 7, 1974).

CONCLUSION

The legal basis for the right to live in the community under equal protection and federal statute as established in *Pennhurst* will be addressed and refined by other federal courts in the months and years ahead as the trials in Connecticut, Kentucky, Michigan, and other states move to conclusion and as the several appeals courts define the reach of Section 504 and related enactments.

Already, on December 13, 1979, the Third Circuit Court of Appeals, *en banc* by a 6 to 3 majority affirmed Judge Broderick's opinion and orders in *Halderman* v. *Pennhurst*, 446 F. Supp. at 1295, holding that under the Developmentally Disabled Assistance and Bill of Rights Act, and under Pennsylvania state law every retarded person has a right to "that education, training and care required by [him] to reach his maximum development"—the right to habilitation—and that these services must be provided in an environment "that is least restrictive on the personal liberties of the retarded."

The Court of Appeals found it unnecessary to consider the Section 504 argument on the constitutional arguments, saying: "[D]einstitutionalization is the favored approach to habilitation, the federal statutory material makes that clear and we acknowledge that constitutional law developments incline in that direction."

Whatever the pace of legal action and the pace of the executive and legislative response to court decisions, the legal principles discussed provide a firm foundation for shaping a future of all retarded people that includes the right to live in the community. The realization of that right depends not so much on its articulation and further refinement by the courts, as it does on the understanding of that right by society and the consistent application of these principles to all programs initiated, supported, and maintained.

REFERENCES

Burt, R. 1976. Beyond the right to rehabilitation. In: M. Kindred, J. Cohen, D. Penrod, and T. Shaffer (eds.), Mentally Retarded Citizens and the Law. President's Committee on Mental Retardation, Washington, D.C.

Goffman, E. 1961. Asylums, XIII. Anchor Books, Garden City, N. Y.

Karst, K. 1977. Equal citizenship under the Fourteenth Amendment. Harv. Law Rev. 91:1, 6.

Index